This City Life

Desmond Mason

Drawings by Joseph W Flack

Edward Arnold

© Desmond Mason and Joseph W. Flack, 1979

First published 1979
by Edward Arnold (Publishers) Ltd
41 Bedford Square
London WC1B 3DQ

British Library Cataloguing in Publication Data
Mason, Desmond
  This city life
  I. Title
  823'.9'1FS   PZ7.M/

  ISBN 0-7131-0344-2

*Text set in 12 on 14 pt Baskerville and printed and bound at
The Camelot Press Ltd, Southampton*

Contents

1 Between the Dole and Work 7
2 Buying a Bike: I 14
3 Buying a Bike: II 20
4 The Waiting Room 26
5 Keeping out of Trouble: I 32
6 Keeping out of Trouble: II 36
7 Disco' at 'The Crown' 42
8 Looking for a Flat – Problems 46
9 Looking for a Flat – Success! 51
10 Job Propects: Attitudes and Interviews 58
11 On Site: Attitudes to Work 62
12 The Interview 69
13 Holiday Preparations 76
14 A Narrow Escape 81
15 Incident at the Youth Club 86
16 Party Preparations 94
17 The Party 100
18 Two Old Men 107
19 Getting into Trouble 114
20 On Holiday in Spain 121

Acknowledgements

I would like to acknowledge the debt
which I owe for much of this material
to the young people employed by the
Community Industry scheme in the London
Borough of Wandsworth. It was my
pleasure to teach them while they were
at a difficult stage in their lives,
and I hope that this book may help
others, some of whom may be at an
equally awkward time, to take from it
something useful. I would also like to thank
the members of the General Studies
team at South Thames College for their
support and co-operation in this project.

To the Student Reading this Book

It is my hope that this book may help you in overcoming certain problems and teach you something about the options that are open to you beyond school or college. I have set the stories in a Community Industry scheme, not because I imagine that all of you will have difficulty in finding work, but because it is an interesting situation: a sort of crossroads between leaving school and finding a regular job. Many of you will, no doubt, find a steady job as soon as you leave school or college. Others among you may find it more difficult, particularly if you have forgotten or neglected many of the things that most employers will expect you to know. You will also find that there are things you need to know which you never thought about until you found yourself having to take your place in the world of work.

What I have tried to do here is teach you something about the things that you may want to know or do in the world away from teaching. I have also tried to explore some of the problems that you may have to face, and situations in which you may find yourself involved. The main aim of the exercises is to polish up your basic English and Maths, but I also intended that in answering the questions to the stories, you may learn some other things that will be useful to you. Good luck anyway.

D. M.

1 Between the Dole and Work

'It's all very well for you,' said Anthony Roach to his friend, Pete Brown. 'You've got a job for the summer, and you've still got another year to go before you leave school. I've been left school for a year now, and my last five months have been spent on the dole. It's just not that easy to find work now, when you got no qualifications from school.'

'It must be a bit depressing,' said Pete. 'What do you have to do to sign on?'

'Well, it ain't much fun, I can tell you that,' Anthony grumbled. 'You only get about twelve quid a week, and the people behind the counter at the Labour Exchange treat you like dirt. Department of Employment? They ought to call it the Department of Unemployment.'

'What do you have to do though? Just sign your name?' Pete asked him again.

'Yeah. More or less. You go through a right load of aggravation first though. You have to fill in a big form, where they ask you all sorts of questions, then they send you over to the Social Security Office. They fill in another bloody great form, then send you back to the Labour Exchange, where they fill in another form, and tell you when to come down and sign on each week. Worst thing of all is the damn great big queues you get everywhere,' Anthony complained. 'Everywhere you go, you have to queue for ages, and everyone is dead miserable and always arguing with the bloke behind the counter.'

'It still sounds like easy money to me,' said Pete.

'I suppose it is really,' Anthony agreed, 'but there isn't much of it, and it don't get you anywhere does it? It gets you down after a bit, joining in the queue with all those dossers and layabouts. It makes you feel like you was one of them.

Know what I mean? I want to learn a trade; do a proper job, and earn a decent bit of money; buy meself a motor-bike and a few decent clothes – not stay on the bloody dole all my life.'

'Our Tommy used to go on like that about it,' said Pete. 'You remember Tommy, don't you? He got a job at a place called Community Industry. He reckons it's all right.'

'What's that then?' Anthony asked him.

'I dunno all that much about it,' Pete answered. 'I think its a place where, if you've been signing on and that, they give you some training to help you stay out of the dole queue.'

'Who runs it?' asked Anthony. 'Is it one these bleeding heart social workers' places?'

'I dunno,' said Pete. 'Our Tommy found out about it from the Careers Office.'

'Yeah?' said Anthony. 'I think I might take a look over there tomorrow and see what they got to offer.'

The next morning, Anthony visited the Careers Office at Clapham Junction. He was interviewed by a pretty young woman who seemed to be genuinely interested in trying to help him. She told him that a number of schemes were available to him in the Wandsworth area, and explained that these schemes differed from place to place, according to where you lived.

The first scheme she explained to him was a college-based course called 'Introduction to Work.' She told him that this course would entitle him to a grant of about £20 per week from the Manpower Services Commission. The course would involve him going to college for up to eighteen weeks, learning basic English and Maths and some basic practical skills. The course would also teach him something about attitudes to work, and how to pass interviews.

'No,' said Anthony. 'I don't want to go back to school, and it's only for eighteen weeks. I was thinking of something that would last a bit longer; something a bit more practical that will really help me to find a proper job.'

'Well,' the Careers Officer said, 'there's always the

Short-Term Employment Project. This lasts from three to six months, and gives you practical experience in things like clerical work or factory work, and you earn a bit more money. Not much more though.'

'Isn't there anything that will last a bit longer?' asked Anthony. 'I want to work somewhere for a good stretch, not just go back onto the dole after a few months'.

'Well, the Job Creation Programme offers work for up to a year,' she replied. 'They pay about £20 per week to lads of your age for doing Council work. Cleaning up parks; doing up houses; all that sort of thing.'

'That don't sound very clever either,' said Anthony after a bit. 'I want to learn a trade, see?'

'A year with the Job Creation Programme *will* show an employer that you *can* work properly, and that you understand the kind of discipline that work involves,' the Careers Officer replied.

Anthony stayed silent.

After a pause, the Careers Officer said, 'If you're really interested in finding work that will help you get a job, you can always try the Industrial Training Workshops. These provide you with a basic trade training in an area like electrics or mechanics, and the chances of finding employment after one of these course is quite good. There is also the possibility of day-release from work, once you have found a job, to do a City and Guilds course at College, where you can gain a proper qualification in your chosen field.'

Anthony was a bit doubtful. 'I'm not much good at school subjects and technical things,' he said. 'How long does the course last?'

'Eighteen weeks,' the Careers Officer replied. 'If you want something that will last longer, the Work Experience Programme could find a place for you. They train you in factory work, office work, shop work – things like that. After six months or so, if you're interested, and if the firm that you've been working for wants you, they can offer you a

9

full-time job on a permanent basis. While you're training, you get £16 per week.'

'Haven't you got anything like painting and decorating that I could learn?' Anthony asked her.

'Yes,' she replied. 'You could try Community Industry.'

'What's that then?' Anthony asked her.

'Community Industry is for people who, because of personal problems or lack of qualifications, are finding it especially difficult to find work,' she explained.

Anthony grinned at her. 'That sounds like me,' he said.

'The Community Industry programme provides work for up to one year,' the Careers Officer continued. 'You work in gangs of eight or ten trainees, with each gang under the supervision of a scheme consultant. These are skilled tradesmen, such as carpenters, painters, bricklayers; and on the female side, sewing machinists, typists; people like that. There are Community Industry Schemes operating in towns all over the country now. The idea is that you learn something of a trade, working on community and environmental projects that would not otherwise be done.'

'What kind of projects?' asked Anthony.

'Doing up old houses that would otherwise be left derelict; painting up old people's houses and homes; landscaping waste ground; insulating houses: all the kind of work connected with the building trade. Mind you,' she said, 'there's no guarantee that you'll find work of a similar kind once you leave Community Industry.'

'It still sounds like just the crack to me,' said Anthony. 'How much do they pay?'

'The pay is rather good,' the Careers Officer replied. 'You get £29.80 per week at seventeen, but I should warn you that the authorities are trying to reduce these wages. They say it's too much.'

'Great!' exclaimed Anthony. 'Can I go and see them?'

'I'll make an appointment for you,' the Careers Officer replied. She smiled at him. 'Thank goodness we found something that suits you,' she said. 'I was beginning to think you were a hopeless case.'

Anthony smiled back at her. 'Thanks for all your help, Miss,' he said. 'Sorry if I've been a bit awkward like.' Encouraged by her smile, he asked her, 'Would you like to come for a cup of coffee?'

She gathered her papers together and looked at him. At first she looked rather stern, then she smiled at him once again. 'No thank you,' she said, 'I don't think my boyfriend would like it.'

Anthony left the Careers Office with a face as red as a beetroot.

Two weeks later, Anthony Roach started work with Community Industry as a part of a painting and decorating team. Within another month he had enough to put down a deposit on a motor-bike.

Questions

1 For how long had Anthony been signing on the dole and how much money does he receive?
2 What is the 'aggravation' that Anthony goes through before he starts getting his dole money?
3 What reasons does Anthony give for not liking signing on, even though he admits it's 'easy money?'
4 What kind of things does Anthony want do to?
5 How did Tommy find out about Community Industry?
6 How much money would Anthony earn altogether if he spent 18 weeks on the 'Introduction to Work' course?
7 What kind of things would he learn on this course?
8 Why isn't Anthony interested in this course?
9 Describe the Short Term Employment Project.
10 What kind of work is offered by the Job Creation Programme and how would it help Anthony find a job afterwards?
11 Describe what the Industrial Training Workshops offer young people.
12 How much would Anthony earn if he spent 26 weeks on the Work Experience Programme?

13 What kind of people is Community Industry specially intended for?
14 What would a working gang consist of at Community Industry?
15 Describe some of the work projects carried out by C.I. (Community Industry).
16 How much would Anthony earn in 26 weeks at C.I.?
17 What is the main drawback of working at C.I.?
18 Which of the options that are offered to Anthony would you choose? Give your reasons for this choice.

            *   *   *

A Do you think that more should be done for young people who leave school and find themselves unemployed? Can you think of any other schemes that could be useful in helping unemployed young people?
B Why is it that unemployment hits young people leaving school especially hard in the present economic climate? What kind of things could be done by Industry to improve the situation?
C Describe your ideal job and the training or qualifications that you would need to obtain it.

2 Buying a Bike: I

Anthony Roach sweated beneath his leather jacket as he looked in the windows of the motor-cycle sales rooms just along the road from Wandsworth Town station. The sun was shining down brilliantly upon a hot Saturday morning, and Anthony wished that he'd left his jacket at home. Still, as he was looking for a motor-bike, he wanted to look the part. His wallet bulged uncomfortably in his back pocket. In the four weeks that he had been at Community Industry, he'd managed to save thirty pounds, and his father had lent him another thirty. He was hoping to buy a second-hand bike on H.P., but all the ones that he had seen so far had been much too expensive. Some of them were £400 and £500, secondhand!

One motor-cycle in the window of the shop caught his eye and held it. It was a smart-looking Suzuki 125 cc, with a price tag on the windscreen offering it at £270. After looking at it carefully, Anthony walked into the shop for a closer look. The salesman came up behind him as he was examining it.

'Good little bike that,' said the salesman. 'It's going at a very fair price too, for a 1975 model.'

'How would I set about getting H.P. on it then?' asked Anthony.

'You have to put down a 15% deposit first of all,' the salesman replied.

'How much is that then?' Anthony asked him.

'That depends on how much the price is going to be,' the salesman answered. 'Have you passed your test?'

'No,' said Anthony, 'but I thought the price was £270.'

'You have to be insured before you can buy a bike off us on H.P.' the salesman explained. 'How old are you?'

'Seventeen,' Anthony replied. 'How much is the insurance?'

The salesman consulted a little notebook from his inside pocket. 'That will cost you another £95 for a third party, fire and theft insurance policy for a year.'

Anthony was flabbergasted. 'How much?' he said. 'I haven't got ninety-five quid.'

'That can go on the H.P. agreement as well,' the salesman explained. 'You can get everything you need on H.P. here: Road Tax; crash helmet; even a couple of accessories if you wanted them.'

'How much is Road Tax?' asked Anthony.

'That's another fiver,' the salesman told him. 'Then there's your crash-helmet.' He indicated a shelf displaying various types of helmet and asked, 'Which of those do you fancy?'

Anthony picked out a brilliant blue space helmet type, and was shocked to hear the price – £22.50! 'Ah well,' he said after a moment, 'I might as well have the one I fancy. I'm going to make myself skint anyway.'

The salesman added up all the figures and worked out the total amount that Anthony wanted to buy on credit. It was a sizeable sum of money. 'You'll have to put down fifteen per cent of that lot,' the salesman told him, after he had explained how much the total was. 'Have you got it?'

'Yeah, I've got it all right,' said Anthony, feeling a bit put out.

'Right,' said the salesman, scribbling away on a pad, 'take the deposit away from the total, then we work out the interest on the balance left to pay. Our interest rate is eighteen per cent per year on what you owe. Do you want to pay it over one or two years?'

'Two, I think,' replied Anthony. 'I don't reckon I could manage it in just one year.'

The salesman talked to himself as he scribbled away on his pad. 'That's eighteen per cent times two . . . plus the balance . . . over twenty-four months . . .' He looked up. 'That's roughly a fiver a week.'

Anthony brightened up. 'Can I put the deposit down now then?'

'Sure,' the salesman replied. 'That will keep the bike for you; and it's always refundable if anything goes wrong.'

'What do you mean "goes wrong"? What can go wrong?' Anthony asked.

'Well, first of all, I have to check some of your personal details, and then make sure that the deal is acceptable to the finance company that is lending the money.'

'Oh,' said Anthony, feeling rather lost in all this financial talk. He handed over the deposit, and tucked the receipt that he was given into his wallet.

'Right,' said the salesman, holding his pen over a bright yellow form, 'you need someone to guarantee you, so that if you fail to repay the loan, the person who guarantees you will have to pay it. It's a kind of insurance for the finance company. Usually it's the father who acts as guarantor for a young chap like you.'

Anthony wasn't sure that he liked being called 'a young chap,' but he decided that it was better than being called 'kid.'

'Yeah,' he said. 'I s'pose my dad'll do it.'

'O.K. Let's start with a few details about you, then I'd like you to answer a few questions about your father.' He went on to ask Anthony all sorts of questions about himself: things like the kind of job he had; how long he'd been there; the name and address of his employer; what he'd been doing before he went there; what kind of place he lived in. Anthony just about managed to answer them, but when it came to answering questions about his father, he found himself stuck. He didn't know the name and address of his father's employer. He didn't know his father's age, and he was very embarrassed to find that he wasn't even sure of his father's name!

'I think it's Trevor,' he said, 'but it might be Eddy.'

The salesman rolled his eyes up to the ceiling and put down his pen. Anthony suddenly remembered that he had a telephone number in his wallet where he could reach his dad at work. He was thankful to recall that his father had gone to work that morning for a bit of Saturday overtime. He gave the salesman the number, and the salesman got through to his father on the 'phone.

Anthony was relieved to hear his father agree to act as his guarantor, and he listened to the crackle of the 'phone as his father answered the salesman's questions. The telephone conversation finally came to an end, and the salesman put the phone down and turned to Anthony with a smile.

'You might be interested to know,' he said, 'that your father's name is Terry.'

Anthony blushed and felt stupid.

'That's that for now then,' the salesman said. 'I'll send this off to the finance company for their approval, and if you can come back with your father on Wednesday evening, you can both sign the H.P. agreement. We'll be open until seven o'clock. O.K.?'

'Yeah. All right then,' said Anthony.

'One more thing,' said the salesman, just as Anthony was about to leave the shop, 'don't forget that you'll have to pay another £95 for your insurance policy for next year. You'll have to save a couple of quid a week towards that if you don't want to get caught out.'

'Thanks a lot mate,' Anthony replied. 'That's a nice cheerful thought.'

He walked back out into the sunshine feeling rather disappointed. He had hoped that he would be able to take his bike away that same day. Trudging towards Wandsworth Town station, he watched a youth go blaring through the traffic on a zippy little bike similar to the one that he'd just put a deposit on. He cheered himself up by imagining himself snarling through the traffic sometime in the not-very-distant future.

Questions

1 How much had Anthony been able to save on average for each week he had been at Community Industry?
2 What is H.P. and how does it work?
3 How much is 15% of the price of the motor-bike?
4 What is the price of the motor-bike, plus the price of insurance?
5 What kind of an insurance policy does the salesman suggest to Anthony, and what does this policy insure against?
6 How much is Road Tax for a motor-cycle?
7 What is the cost of the motor-cycle, plus the cost of insurance, plus the cost of Road Tax, plus the cost of the crash helmet?
8 How much is 15% of this total cost?
9 How much is left for Anthony to pay, once he has put down his 15% deposit?
10 How much is 18% of this amount, multiplied by two?
11 *Exactly* how much money will Anthony have to pay per month?
12 Who does the salesman have to check with before he can agree to sell Anthony the motor-cycle on H.P.?
13 What does the guarantor have to agree to in an H.P. agreement?
14 What kind of questions does the salesman ask Anthony about himself as he fills in the yellow form?
15 What kind of questions does the salesman ask Anthony about his father as he fills in the form?
16 How does Anthony finally manage to put the salesman in touch with his father?
17 What does Anthony have to do on the following Wednesday evening?
18 Why is Anthony disappointed as he leaves the shop?

3 Buying a Bike: II

Anthony was really looking forward to riding his motor-cycle as he returned to the shop with his father on Wednesday evening. He had been thinking of little else but the bike since Saturday, and now, at last, he was going to pick it up.

The salesman had all the papers ready for them when they arrived at the shop at around six-thirty.

'How do you do, Mr. Roach,' said the salesman, shaking hands with Anthony's father. 'Everything is fine as far as the finance company is concerned, so it just remains for you and your son to sign these papers.' He handed them each a copy of a form, keeping two copies back for himself.

'Let's have a look at this bike first,' said Anthony's father.

Anthony felt embarrassed. He didn't think his father knew anything about motor-bikes, and he didn't want to appear awkward after the salesman had been so helpful. 'It's all right, Dad,' he said. 'I've seen the bike. It's O.K.'

'Well let's have a look at it then,' his father replied. 'I'm not giving you money just to buy a load of rubbish that'll kill you as soon as you get on it.'

Anthony reflected that his father wasn't giving him any money at all. He was lending it to him. He didn't say anything though.

The salesman took Anthony and his father out to a large garage at the back of the salesrooms. Anthony saw his bike over at the side of the garage, leaning on its stand looking bright and zippy.

Anthony's father looked the bike over carefully. 'What's the bike's top speed?' he asked.

'It's got eighty on the clock,' the salesman replied, 'but seventy-five is about the most she'd manage.'

'Blimey!' exclaimed Anthony's father. 'That's a bit strong for a little thing like that isn't it? The top speed on the old Bantam I started off on was about fifty – and that was going down hill with the wind behind me!'

'I started off on a Tiger Cub,' said the salesman. 'Now that was a little bike with a lot of poke.'

Anthony listened in surprise as his father and the salesman discussed the old British motor-cycles that used to dominate the market. He had never realised that his father knew anything about bikes at all.

'Yeah, those were the days,' said the salesman. 'It's all these little Japanese jobs these days. Mind you, they're pretty good, and they make some classy big bikes too.'

'Start this 'un up then, and let's have a listen,' said Anthony's father.

The salesman switched on the petrol and the ignition, and the little bike started first time, revving smoothly as he turned back the throttle.

'She sounds fair enough,' said Anthony's father, speaking above the noise of the engine. 'It's a bit fast for a learner in London traffic though, isn't it?'

'No it's not,' Anthony protested. 'Some of my mates have got much bigger bikes, and they're only learners.'

The salesman switched the engine off and spoke in the sudden silence.

'We always advise a first-time bike-buyer to take a training course in riding a motor-cycle before he goes out onto the road. It's a fact that a large number of accidents involving motor-bikes take place within hours of the bike being bought.'

Anthony sensed a new obstacle coming between him and his bike, and he said quickly, 'Aw come on, Dad. I'll be all right.'

His father ignored him. 'Where do these courses run then?' he asked.

'Wimbledon Stadium has a four hour training course on their track on Saturday morning. As a part of our service, we pay your son's fee for the course, and we'll take his bike over there for him to pick it up then.'

'Great!' said Anthony's father. 'We'll sign those papers now. What time does the course start?'

'Nine o'clock,' replied the salesman.

'We'll be there,' Mr. Roach told him. 'He can take the bike after that. You'll get it over there will you?'

'You leave it to us, sir,' said the salesman. He smiled. 'After all, we don't want our customers ending up in hospital. They can't pay us then!'

Anthony signed the papers gloomily, and left the shop with his father. Walking back to the station, he felt disappointed and frustrated. Would he ever get to ride his bike?

The two days seemed to pass with incredible slowness, but finally Saturday morning arrived, and the moment came when he was sitting astride his bike and listening to the voice of the instructor. Then, at last, he felt his bike moving under him, and he was watching through the visor of his crash helmet as the track slid past him. As his confidence grew, he moved faster and faster, slipping through the other riders and taking the lead. 'This is dead easy,' he thought to himself. Then he realised that he had come into a bend too fast, and he felt himself lose control of the machine as it slid away beneath him. He banged his elbows and his hips painfully on the ground and felt very stupid. He was the first learner to come off his bike that morning, and he felt that the others were all laughing at him. He also felt that he'd let himself down in front of his father. He picked himself up and limped anxiously over to his bike, blushing beneath his crash helmet. Luckily, the bike seemed all right. The engine was still running and Anthony picked it up in order to get back on it. But he didn't notice that the back wheel was still being driven by the engine, and as soon as the rear wheel touched the ground and gripped, the bike shot off, dragging Anthony across the track until he fell over once again!

The instructor came running up to him. After making sure that he was not hurt, the instructor told him, 'Always remember to switch off your bike before you pick it up if you fall off it. Imagine what would have happened if this was a main road. If you hadn't been run over by something where you fell, your bike might have dragged you straight under a 'bus when you tried to pick it up. I lost a mate like that.'

The other learners were gathered around listening carefully. Anthony wished that it had happened to someone else rather than him. Still, he was glad it hadn't happened on the road, and his bike was still intact.

The instructor continued talking. 'Always remember,' he said, 'that the road is a dangerous place, and a motor-bike isn't just a toy. You have to learn how to handle it safely, and treat it with respect. You have to learn how it accelerates and how it brakes; how far you can lean it over before you lose control when you're cornering, and how fast you can accelerate when you're overtaking. You have to learn to think fast and react fast, because you're moving a lot faster than you realise. Showing off is a good way to have an accident.'

The lesson continued until one o'clock. Anthony came off his bike three more times during the morning, but others came off four or five times. One boy gave up and left, leaving his bike to be picked up by the dealer from whom he was going to buy it. At the end of the morning Anthony felt that he could handle his bike with reasonable skill. He didn't like to think what might have happened if he'd just gone straight out onto the busy main roads.

'Good luck son. Drive carefully,' said his father, as Anthony prepared to move off into the traffic outside the stadium.

'Don't worry. I'll be all right,' Anthony replied.

Ten minutes later, sandwiched between two lorries as he made his way round a one-way system, Anthony was very thankful he had taken the introductory course, especially when a car moved across his path without indicating. He

looked over at the enormous spinning wheels of the lorry beside him; at the solid metal edges of the car in front of him; and at the threatening face of the van that loomed up in his rear-view mirror. He realised how fragile and small a motor-cycle is on the road. Yes, he was glad he'd taken those lessons.

Questions

1 What does Anthony's father want to do before he signs the papers?
2 Why is Anthony embarrassed by his father's request?
3 What was the top speed of Mr. Roach's old 'Bantam'?
4 What worries Mr. Roach about Anthony's motor-cycle?
5 What fact does the salesman tell them about accidents involving motor-cycles?
6 How long does the training course at Wimbledon last, and when does it take place?
7 How will Anthony's bike get over to Wimbledon?
8 Why does the salesman not want customers to end up in hospital?
9 What is the first thing that Anthony does wrong when he begins to ride his motor-cycle?
10 What is the second thing that he does wrong?
11 How did the instructor lose a friend of his?
12 Why is it necessary to think fast and react fast on a motor-cycle?
13 What does the instructor say that showing off can lead to?
14 What incident happens to make Anthony glad that he had taken the introductory training course?
15 What does Anthony realise as he drives through the traffic?

*　　　*　　　*

A Do you think that it is worthwhile to buy things on H.P.? What kind of things would you buy if you had the chance? Work out how much they would cost altogether, and find out how much interest you would pay on them at eighteen per cent over two years.
B Do you think it did Anthony some good to have to wait before he got what he wanted? Give reasons for your opinion.

4 The Waiting Room

Tommy Brown and his cousin Jimmy were on their way home from seeing a horror film neither of them had enjoyed, as they had been both scared and depressed by it. As they walked through the darkness in the drizzling rain towards Wandsworth Town station, they discussed the film.

'It was just a load of rubbish,' said Tommy. 'All that guff about the devil and the end of the world. I don't know why they make films like that.'

'Well, it's the money isn't it?' replied Jimmy. 'They just make films that will cause a lot of aggravation and get in the papers, then everyone goes to see them to see how 'orrible they are.'

'Yeah,' agreed Tommy, 'but I wish I 'adn't bothered. I'd sooner have had a couple of pints.' They turned into the tunnel that led to the station, and climbed up the steps to the platform for Clapham Junction. When they reached the top, they showed their tickets to the inspector and went into the waiting-room. The wall clock said it was eleven o'clock.

A man was sitting in the corner of the room, down by the fire, with a blanket wrapped around him. He was unshaven and poorly dressed, and he looked pale and ill. He looked towards the youths and asked them, in a surprisingly 'posh' voice, to close the door. Jimmy shut the door, and the three of them were closed in together in a rather strained silence.

'Take a seat by the fire,' offered the man, as though it was his home. 'The devil knows its cold enough.'

Jimmy and Tommy sat down opposite him. 'Yeah,' said Tommy, 'it is pretty cold.' He looked at the man's threadbare, dirty clothes, his muddy shoes, and his trousers tucked into his socks, and he hoped that he would never be like that.

'My wife gave me this blanket,' volunteered the man. 'She said that it was so cold, I should take a blanket from the car.'

'Yeah,' said Jimmy after a moment of silence, 'well, it certainly is cold.' Privately he thought that the blanket was too filthy to have come from a car, but he said nothing.

The man drank something from a paint tin by the side of him. 'I've been working hard today,' he said, 'and when I've been working, I like a drink.'

There was a silence.

'My wife didn't want me to work today,' said the man. 'She said it was too cold. But I've been commissioned to do it. My daughters are both scientists. Brilliant. Oh, I love my daughters. And they love me. They said to me in hospital, "Daddy, we think you're the most wonderful man in the world." I had a heart attack you know. I was supposed to die. I was supposed to be dead.'

Tommy and Jimmy looked at him in silence. Their silence seemed to anger the man.

'Dead,' he repeated. 'I was supposed to be dead, do you hear?'

'You seem all right now,' said Jimmy.

'What happened then?' asked Tommy. Both of them were longing for the train to come so that they could get away from this peculiar man.

'I was supposed to be dead,' repeated the man moodily. 'Do you believe in life after death?'

'I . . . I don't know,' replied Tommy.

'I've seen it,' said the man. 'I could tell you a thing or two. How would you like to die? What would be your ideal death? Would you like to be shot? Die in bed? Get run over? Be poisoned? Strangled?' He was staring at them, his bloodshot eyes wide open, flickering from one of them to the other. His top lip was twitching. 'I've seen men die. Plenty of them. And I've killed men. Killed them all ways. They twitch as they're dying. I've seen men walking around with their brains dripping out.' He looked at the apprehensive faces of the two youths sitting opposite him and grinned wolfishly. 'You're not scared are you?' he sneered. 'You're not frightened of death are you?'

Tommy suddenly decided that he'd had enough of the man's strange talk. 'Look mate,' he said, 'we're not frightened of you, and I don't know what you're talking about, so just stop trying to be moody. We done nothing to upset you, so stop trying to upset us.'

'Ahhh,' said the man mockingly. 'Am I upsetting you?' He looked at Tommy, his mouth working. He bit his lower lip, then took another drink from the tin beside him. Then he reached into his inside pocket and pulled out a battered wallet. He took from it a rather dog-eared photograph and offered it to Tommy with a strange smile on his face. 'Here sonny,' he said, 'have a look at that.'

Tommy took the photograph and felt his stomach freeze as he looked at it. It showed the man in Army uniform when he was younger. He was holding a rifle with a bayonet in one hand, and with the other he was holding up the severed head of a Chinese. The tongue of the head was poking out, seeming impossibly long, and the bulging eyes were staring into the camera. Tommy's mouth was dry, and his heart was beating fast. He showed his cousin the photo without looking at him, then he handed it back to the man. 'That's horrible,' he said. 'What do you carry that around with you for?' He barely heard the train coming in.

'That's death, sonny,' the man chuckled as he put the photograph back into his wallet.

'Come on Tommy,' said Jimmy. 'The train's in.' He ran for the door, and had some difficulty opening it.

The man lurched to his feet and asked, 'Will you travel with me?'

To their surprise, the train started to pull out almost as soon as it had stopped, the driver obviously thinking that no one was getting on. Tommy and Jimmy ran for the train, and opening the door of a moving carriage, they threw themselves in. The man with the blanket tried to copy them, but fell back onto the platform, the drink from his tin spilling all over him.

Tommy and Jimmy sat down with gasps of relief.

'Thank God we got away from that nutter,' said Tommy. 'He was doing my head in, slinging around all that verbal.'

'He's probably on the run from a mental hospital if you ask me,' volunteered Jimmy. 'What a bloody head case.'

'Anyway,' said Tommy, 'at least it took my mind off that moody film. It seems there's enough to be scared of in the world, without imagining things.'

Both of them were rather disturbed when they read *The Evening News* the following day. It carried a story of a man described as 'an alcoholic psychopath,' who had escaped from Springfield Mental Hospital the previous day. He had apparently killed himself by throwing himself under a passing train from the platform of Wandsworth Town station, AT NINE-THIRTY AT NIGHT!

'Blimey!' said Tommy. 'Do you think it was him?'

'Makes you wonder, dunnit?' replied Jimmy. There was nothing more he could think of to say.

Questions

1 What kind of weather was it as Tommy and Jimmy were walking home?
2 What reason did Jimmy give for the film-makers making films like the one they had seen.
3 Describe the man in the waiting-room.
4 What kind of blanket was the man wrapped in?
5 Do you believe what the man was saying about his family? Give your reasons.
6 What had happened to the man for him to say he should be dead?
7 What time was it as they were talking to him?
8 Did Tommy and Jimmy enjoy talking to the man?

9 What do Tommy and Jimmy do that seems to anger the man?
10 What does the man say that people do as they're dying?
11 What does the man suggest that Tommy and Jimmy are scared of?
12 What does the man say that the photograph shows?
13 What is the last question that Tommy asks the man?
14 What is the last request that the man makes of Tommy and Jimmy?
15 What happens to the man when he tries to jump on the moving train?
16 What does Jimmy think of the man after they have got away from him?
17 What does Tommy say that meeting the man did for him?
18 How did the newspaper describe the man?
19 What does Jimmy mean when he says, 'It makes you wonder?'

*   *   *

A Try writing a story of your own about a supernatural or frightening event.
B Write a story beginning, 'The wind howled around the old house on the hill, as the trees swayed backwards and forwards, and the clouds swirled across the face of the moon. . .'
C Write an essay entitled: 'Why do people believe in ghosts?'
D Write an essay describing the different types of things that people are scared of.

5 Keeping out of Trouble: I

'Did you know that Lorna Black has got herself pregnant?' Mandy Sloane said to her friend Sandra Carter one morning, as the two girls settled down to another day's work in the sewing shop at Community Industry.

'She hasn't has she?' exclaimed Sandra. 'She's only been going out with that boy Colin for a few months!'

'I know,' replied Mandy, 'but that doesn't seem to have stopped her.'

'How did you find out?' asked Sandra. 'Did she tell you herself?'

'Not in so many words,' Mandy replied, 'but I saw her and Colin last night. They both looked so miserable that I knew something was wrong. I asked Lorna what was the matter, and she said to ask Colin.'

'What did Colin say?' Sandra asked.

'He told me to push off and mind my own business, the pig!' said Mandy.

'It don't take much to work out what's wrong with them.'

'You'd think they'd be more careful,' said Sandra.

'Yeah,' said Mandy, 'and that reminds me: I think I want to go on to the pill.'

'I've been on it for ages,' Sandra told her. 'What have you been using?'

'I get Winston to use a sheath,' Mandy replied, 'but he doesn't like it much. He reckons it's like having a haircut with a hat on.'

The two girls laughed. 'I used to use a cap,' Sandra told her friend. 'I changed to the pill though, because my doctor told me that the cap wasn't all that reliable. Not the way I was using it, anyway. It's best to be safe, isn't it?'

'Does the pill have any bad side effects?' Mandy asked her. 'I've heard that it can make you feel terrible, or even give you heart attacks!'

'Well, it hasn't had any bad effects on me,' Sandra replied. 'Anyway, if you go along to the doctor, he'll tell you all about it.'

'Yes, I think I'll make an appointment,' said Mandy thoughtfully. 'I don't want to end up like Lorna Black.'

A week later, on the day of her appointment with the doctor, Mandy got cold feet.

'I feel too embarrassed to go to the doctor's and tell him I want to go onto the pill,' she told Sandra. 'He'd examine me wouldn't he, you know,' she giggled, 'down there?'

Sandra smiled at her. 'Of course he'll examine you. That's part of what the purpose of going to him is. Anyway,' she continued, 'I'd go along to see him if I was you. Have you heard the latest about Lorna Black?'

'No,' Mandy replied. 'What's happening?'

'It's terrible,' Sandra said, in a voice which suggested that she was enjoying talking about it just the same. 'When Lorna's dad found out she was in the club, he went straight round to Colin's house, and him and Colin's dad had a big fight. Well, Colin's dad beat Mr. Black up, and now Lorna's been kicked out of the house, and her dad says he never wants to see her again.'

'Blimey!' said Mandy. 'Where's she staying now then?'

'She's stopping round at Colin's for the time being,' Sandra told her, 'but now his dad's started going on at her, calling her a slut and all that, and she hates it. She was telling me that Colin's started to go off her as well, blaming her as though it was all her fault.'

'How horrible!' Mandy exclaimed. 'I'd really hate to be in that position.'

'Lorna's talking about having an abortion,' continued Sandra. 'She said that she could get it done on the National Health if she had it done before she's twenty weeks gone.'

'What? That long after?' Mandy asked in amazement.

'The baby must be fully formed by then. I think that's cruel.'
There was a silence for a moment, then Mandy added
thoughtfully, 'It must be ever so painful.'

'I dunno,' Sandra replied, 'I've never had one.' She
paused. 'I think if it was me who got pregnant I'd have it
adopted.'

'I don't know how you could,' protested Mandy. 'Just
think of it: seeing the poor little thing, all small and helpless,
then having to give it to someone else to look after, and
probably never seeing it again.'

'Well I don't agree with abortions,' Sandra declared
firmly. 'I think it's wrong to kill it, once its started to grow
inside you. Having it adopted is better than just killing it and
flushing it down the toilet.'

Mandy was shocked into silence for a minute, then she
said, 'Imagine how you'd feel afterwards. You'd never know
how it had grown up or anything, and if it was a boy, he'd
never know who his proper mum and dad were, and you'd
always wonder if he was happy, or if you had walked past him
in the street and not recognised him. I'm sure I'd never get it
off my mind,' Mandy continued. 'It would be really a
horrible thing to have to live with for the rest of your life.'

'Well, you know what's the best thing to do, don't you?'
said Sandra.

'What?' asked Mandy.

'You want to make sure it doesn't happen by being a bit
careful when you're having it off,' Sandra replied. 'You want
to go along to the doctor's tonight, and stop being so bloody
silly.'

'Yeah. I suppose I should really,' said Mandy
thoughtfully. 'It can't be all that bad. I mean, lots of other
girls do it, don't they?'

Sandra began to sing by way of an answer: 'If you were
the only girl in the world . . .'

'Oh shut up!' said Mandy, laughing. 'I'm going to make
a cuppa. All this talking makes me thirsty.'

34

Questions

1 How long has Lorna Black been going out with her boyfriend?
2 Why does Mandy think that Lorna is pregnant?
3 What does Colin tell Mandy when she asks him what is wrong?
4 What are Winston's objections to using a sheath?
5 Why did Sandra stop using the cap method of contraception?
6 What are the bad side-effects that Mandy has heard about the pill?
7 What is the first thing that Lorna's father does when he finds out that she is pregnant?
8 How do Colin and his father behave towards Lorna when she goes to live with them?
9 What is the maximum number of weeks that Lorna can be pregnant and have an abortion on the National Health?
10 Why does Mandy think it cruel to allow abortions so late in pregnancy?
11 What are Mandy's objections to adoption?
12 What are Sandra's objections to abortion?
13 What is Sandra's advice about avoiding these kinds of problems?
14 Why does Mandy think that it can't be all that bad, after all, to consult the doctor about birth control?

*   *   *

A Do you think that there is anything wrong with having sex before marriage? Give reasons to support your opinion.
B What are the main dangers of promiscuous sex?
C Do you agree with legalised abortion? What are the arguments for and against it?
D Which do you think is preferable, abortion or adoption, or would you never consider either alternative? Give your reasons for your attitude.

6 Keeping out of Trouble: II

It was seven o'clock when Mandy was finally called from the waiting-room into the doctor's surgery. She walked into the antiseptic-smelling surgery feeling nervous and unsure of herself. Even the way she walked seemed strange to her. But as she sat down and began to speak to the doctor, she found much of her embarrassment dissolving. When she explained to him that she wanted to go onto the pill, he didn't seem to be at all put out. It was just as though she had told him that she had a cold or backache.

'I see,' he said. 'Well, first of all I have some questions that I should like to ask you, then I shall give you an internal examination to make sure that everything is all right up inside you. My receptionist, who is also a trained nurse, will assist me in my examination of you. O.K.?'

Mandy felt very shy, and her heart was beating rather fast, but she was relieved by his calm and matter-of-fact approach. 'Yes,' she said shyly.

The doctor smiled at her reassuringly. 'Good,' he said. 'There's nothing for you to worry about. Just relax while I ask you some questions.' He held his pen poised over a sheet of paper and asked her, 'Have you ever been on the pill before?'

'No,' Mandy replied, watching the doctor making a note from her reply.

'Have you or any of your family ever suffered from diabetes or heart trouble?'

'No,' said Mandy. 'At least, I don't think so. None of our family has, but I don't know about my uncles and aunts and that.'

'That's fine,' he said, writing as he spoke. 'Do you or any of your family suffer from high blood pressure or thrombosis?'

Mandy pulled a face. 'I don't think so,' she said. 'Most of our family are pretty healthy.'

'Good,' said the doctor, rising to his feet. 'Now, just take off your cardigan and we'll weigh you, then take your blood pressure.'

After being weighed Mandy took off her cardigan and watched as the doctor slipped a rubber tube around her upper arm, and then squeezed a rubber bulb until the tube tightened. The doctor looked at a gauge attached to the appliance, then made another note on his pad. 'Good. That's fine,' he said, smiling at her as he removed the tube from her arm. He walked across the room and pressed a buzzer on his desk. He spoke into a microphone connected to the reception desk. 'Come into the surgery please, Mrs. Hudson,' he said. Then he moved over to the wash basin in the corner of the room and began to wash his hands.

The receptionist came in almost straight away. She was a bright, efficient-looking woman in her late thirties. She smiled at Mandy as she came up to the doctor's desk.

Turning from the sink, the doctor began to dry his hands. 'Would you prepare Miss Sloane for an internal please, Mrs. Hudson?' he said.

The receptionist turned to Mandy. 'Come over here, dear,' she said, indicating a table and screen over by the wall. 'If you slip off your tights and panties behind the screen, then the Doctor can examine you while you're lying on the examining table.'

Mandy did as she was told, and felt herself blushing as she lay down on the plastic covered surface of the table. The receptionist smiled at her reassuringly. As the doctor approached the table, Mandy saw that he was wearing a plastic glove on one hand. She shut her eyes. She felt her knees being raised gently, then heard the doctor's voice.

'What I'm going to do now,' he said, 'is take a little smear from up inside you, just to test that you're free from any infection. Try and relax now. This won't take a second.'

Mandy felt something metallic holding her open as the

doctor took a sample from inside her vagina. It was quite painless, and seemed to take only a minute. She was relieved to feel the pressure inside her ease, and she opened her eyes as the doctor said, 'There you are. That's all over now. Sit up please.'

The doctor moved over to the sink, throwing the plastic glove in a rubbish bin. Then he washed his hands while the receptionist sealed the specimen they had taken from Mandy into a container. Mandy put her underclothes back on.

'Now,' said the doctor as he dried his hands, 'there's just one more thing. I want to check your breasts to make sure there are no growths that we have to worry about. Would you take off your bra please?' Mandy did as she was asked, and was surprised to find that she didn't feel embarrassed at all as the doctor went round to the back of her and carefully felt around her breasts with the tips of his fingers. She was glad that the receptionist was there though.

'Righto,' said the doctor. 'That's that out of the way. Nothing to worry about there. You can get dressed now.' He went over to his desk and sat down, where he wrote some notes onto a card in front of him. When Mandy was fully dressed again, he said to his receptionist, 'Thank you, Mrs. Hudson. That's it for now.' He looked over at Mandy. 'Come and sit down Miss Sloane,' he said.

As Mandy sat down, the receptionist left the room, and the doctor began to talk to her.

'Now,' said the doctor, placing the tips of his fingers together, 'before you go any further with this, I should explain to you how the pill works. It promotes the flow of a hormone called oestrogen, and this prevents the egg from fertilising in your ovaries. Your periods will continue regularly, but you won't be actually fertile until you stop taking the pill. Do you follow me so far?'

'I think so,' said Mandy. 'Does that mean that as soon as I start taking the pill, I'll be sterile?'

'No,' replied the doctor. 'You have to take ordinary

precautions against conception for the first month. It's not really safe until after you've been on it for a month. Now,' he paused. 'This is most important, and I must stress it. You must remember to take the pill that I prescribe for you EVERY DAY WITHOUT FAIL, because if you miss a day, you upset the cycle, and it can stop the drug from working, with the result that you get pregnant.'

'But is it really reliable if I do take it every day?' asked Mandy.

'That is the main advantage of it as a method of contraception,' the doctor replied. 'As long as you remember to take it every day, the pill is ninety-nine point nine per cent reliable.' He smiled at her as he continued, 'It also has other advantages. It will improve the tone of your skin, and make your periods completely regular and less uncomfortable.'

'Sounds great,' said Mandy.

'There can be less pleasant side effects though,' said the doctor seriously. 'You may find that you put on weight or that you get particularly depressed around the time of your period. Alternatively, you may find that you get headaches, or start to feel nauseous. If you feel any of these adverse effects, and if they persist after the first month, you should come and see me to see if your pill needs to be changed.'

'My friend hasn't had any of those,' said Mandy, feeling a bit put off.

'A lot of women don't,' replied the doctor. 'I'm just telling you, so that if you do, you'll know what to do.' He paused. 'You remember I asked you about illnesses in the family earlier on?' he asked.

'What, about heart trouble and blood pressure and that?' replied Mandy.

'That's it,' said the doctor. 'There is a slight risk that taking the pill can bring on these conditions, and if there is any history of these illnesses in the family, that risk is somewhat higher. Do you understand me?'

'How big is the risk?' asked Mandy, feeling a bit scared.

'It isn't a very high risk,' he replied, 'but it is still a risk.' He paused. 'Well,' he said finally, 'after hearing all that, do you still want to go onto the pill? That's the big question you must ask yourself now.' He looked at her in silence for a moment, then he added gently, 'There are other methods, you know.'

Mandy thought for a while, then she said, 'Is the pill the safest one?'

'All forms of contraception carry a certain risk,' the doctor replied. 'On balance, however, the pill is probably the most reliable form of contraception that we have discovered, short of permanent sterilisation.'

Mandy giggled nervously. 'I wouldn't want that,' she said. 'I think I'd like to go on the pill, doctor, if you think I'll be all right.'

The doctor smiled at her. 'From all of your answers to my questions, and from my examination of you, I don't imagine it will do you any harm.' He scribbled something onto the prescription pad in front of him. 'I'm going to give you a three month supply of pills, and I'd like you to come back in three months for another check-up, and then we'll give you some more if everything is O.K.' he said.

'Thank you, doctor,' Mandy replied, feeling relieved that it was all over at last.

The doctor finished writing on the pad, and handed her the prescription. 'If you can't come back here, or if you'd prefer not to,' he said, 'you can always go along to your local Family Planning Association Clinic when your three months is up. They'll give you a proper check-up and any further advice you may want.'

'Thank you very much,' said Mandy, taking the prescription and putting it in her purse. She walked to the door of the surgery which the doctor was standing by.

'Just before you go,' he said, 'let me remind you again. You must take these pills every day, or they won't work properly. Don't forget,' he held the door open for her, 'EVERY DAY'.

Mandy walked away from the doctor's through the

evening sunlight with his final words ringing in her ears: 'Every day . . . every day.' It reminded her of a song that she couldn't quite remember.

Questions

1 How did the doctor respond when Mandy told him that she wanted to go onto the pill?
2 Name four of the illnesses that the doctor asks Mandy about.
3 Why does the doctor ask his receptionist to come into the surgery?
4 Why does the doctor take a smear from Mandy?
5 How long does the internal examination seem to take?
6 What special article does the doctor wear to make the internal examination?
7 What kind of external examination does he make, and why?
8 What is the name of the hormone that the doctor describes?
9 How does this hormone work?
10 For how long must Mandy take the pill before it is safe?
11 What are the advantages of going onto the pill?
12 What may the unpleasant side-effects of taking the pill be?
13 What should Mandy do about these side-effects if they affect her?
14 What are the illnesses that taking the pill might bring on?
15 How great is the risk of these illnesses happening?
16 How reliable is the pill as a method of contraception?
17 What does the doctor tell Mandy to do after three months?
18 What is Mandy's alternative to returning to the doctor?
19 What is the thing that the doctor emphasises most about taking the pill?

        *   *   *

A How many different methods of contraception do you know of? Make a list of them, grading them in their order of reliability.
B If people wish to avoid having children, should the male take an equal responsibility with the female to avoid conception? What kinds of precaution can the male take?
C What would you do if you found that you, or your girlfriend, were pregnant? What do you think your parents would do?
D Do people look down on unmarried mothers or illegitimate children? Why?
E What are the disadvantages of giving birth to an unwanted child? What bad effects might it have on child and parents?

7 Disco' at 'The Crown'

Winston Lewis and his friend Tommy Brown were on their way over to Clapham Junction for the night. There was a discotheque on over at 'The Crown,' and as Winston's girlfriend Mandy was spending the night with her friend over in Balham, Winston and Tommy had decided to have a 'lads' night out together. Both of them were looking forward to a couple of beers, a good dance, and who knows but maybe some beautiful young lady might come along for one or other of them – maybe even two beautiful young ladies!

The first bit of trouble they had that night was on the bus to Clapham. A couple of 'Teddy Boys' in long drape coats and tight trousers got on the bus and sat in the seat behind them. One of them poked Tommy in the back. Tommy turned around rather angrily, and felt his stomach turn at the sight of the mean, pimply face that was staring fiercely into his.

'Got a light, punk?' said the 'Ted.'

'No,' said Tommy, and turned away, hoping that he would be left in peace. Winston was the next to be poked in the back.

'Got a light, blackie?' the 'Ted' asked again.

'Who are you talking to?' Winston demanded angrily as he turned to face his tormentor.

'You,' said the 'Ted.' 'Do you want to make something of it?'

Two big men sitting on the other side of the aisle leaned towards the quarrelling youths. One of them, a stocky man in a donkey jacket said to the 'Ted,' 'Listen chum, if you want any trouble, just get off the bus and I'll kick your teeth down your throat.'

The 'Ted' went pale. 'Leave it out,' he said. 'I was only messing around.'

'Well save your messing around for another time,' said the man. 'The bus isn't the place for it.'

The two 'Teds' got off at the next stop, and the rest of the journey was uneventful.

When they got to the pub, the disco was in full swing. The two youths moved through the crowded bar up to the counter, where they ordered a couple of pints of lager. As they gulped thirstily at their drinks, Winston remarked, 'You know, those "Teds" are a lot of harassment to everybody. They cause trouble wherever they go. I nearly had a fight on that bus, you know.'

'Yeah,' Tommy agreed, 'I nearly smacked that bloke right in the mouth. He was lucky I didn't.'

'I could see you were getting angry,' said Winston. 'I don't like people to talk to me like that. It's out of order.'

The two of them moved to the edge of the dance floor.

Two pretty girls were dancing in front of them. Tommy nudged his friend. 'I don't like yours,' he said.

Winston and Tommy moved onto the dance floor and started dancing with the two girls. After dancing their way through a few records, they moved off the dance floor and took the girls up to the bar for a drink. Soon they were all deep in conversation. Winston was cuddling up to his dancing partner in a corner of the bar when he suddenly felt a sharp dig in the ribs. This was followed by a kick in the back of his leg. Winston turned around to find Mandy staring furiously up at him.

'Who's this, then?' said Mandy spitefully.

'Oh no,' groaned Winston. He moved away from his new companion, and with Mandy following him, left the pub.

Tommy ran up to them just outside the door of the pub.

'Hi, Mandy,' he said. 'Are you shooting off Winston?' he asked his friend.

'Yes he is shooting off, Tommy Brown,' said Mandy. 'You encouraged him to come down here two-timing me. You're as bad as he is.'

'Aw come on, Mandy,' said Winston. 'I was only having a dance.'

'I'll see you tomorrow, Winston. Bye, Mandy,' said Tommy, and he vanished back into the pub.

'Yes,' said Mandy. 'It looked like you was just dancing,' and she began to cry.

'Come to that,' said Winston, 'What were you doing in that disco if you weren't looking for blokes?'

Mandy stopped crying and looked up at Winston.

'Oh well. Let's forget it,' she said. She snuggled up to him and said, 'Come on. Let's go over to "The Plough" and have a drink.'

'Fair enough,' replied Winston, and they walked off together in the glow of the street lamps and the headlights of the passing cars.

Questions

1 Why were Winston and Tommy going over to Clapham Junction?
2 Where was Mandy supposed to be going for the night?
3 What were Winston and Tommy looking forward to that night?
4 Why did Tommy turn around on the bus?
5 How did Tommy feel when he saw the 'Teds?'
6 How did the 'Teds' insult Tommy and Winston?
7 Who stopped the quarrel, and how?
8 What did Winston say that 'Teds' always did?
9 What did Tommy say that he nearly did?
10 Do you think he was telling the truth? Give your reasons.
11 What did Tommy say when he saw the two girls dancing?
12 How was Winston suddenly attacked?
13 What did Winston do when he saw Mandy?
14 Why was Mandy angry with Tommy?
15 How did Winston stop Mandy crying?

❄   ❄   ❄

A Do you blame Winston and Tommy for having a 'lads' night out? Give your reasons.
B What would you have done if you were on the bus with Winston and Tommy?
C What would you do if you caught (or were yourself caught by) your 'steady' partner 'two-timing' at a disco?

8 Looking for a Flat-Problems

'I had another row with my Mum last night,' Mandy Sloane told her boyfriend Winston. 'She's been getting on at me something wicked lately.'

'What was it this time?' asked Winston, 'Didn't you feed the budgie?'

'Very funny,' said Mandy. 'Actually she was moaning that I never help around the house. It's just not true. I always do the washing up after tea.'

'Yeah. Well, that must help a lot,' said Winston.

They were sitting together in a snack bar, having a cup of coffee passing the time before they went on to watch a film.

'I'm fed up with it at home,' Mandy grumbled. 'What with Mum going on at me all the time, and Dad grizzling about the time I get in at night. It gets on my nerves.'

'Why don't you get a place of your own then?' Winston asked her. 'You're old enough to please yourself where you live.'

'I'd like to,' she replied 'but it would be too expensive wouldn't it? I don't think I could afford it on my money.'

'Course you could,' said Winston. 'It's just a matter of luck, girl. Anyway, you could always share a place with someone else. There are plenty of places for people who want to share.'

'How do you mean?' asked Mandy.

'Well, my brother Archie is living in a house with a lot of other people and they all pay the rent between them and if someone moves out, they have an empty room to let,' Winston explained.

'I wouldn't fancy that,' said Mandy, 'living with a lot of people who I didn't know.'

'Archie says he makes a lot of friends living like that,' replied Winston. 'Well, if you don't fancy that, why don't you get one of your friends to rent a place with you?'

'How do you find all these places anyway?' asked, Mandy, changing the subject.

'In the papers and magazines,' Winston replied. 'You find them in shop windows too. The shop windows and the local papers are the best for finding somewhere in your own neighbourhood. At least,' he continued, 'that's what Archie said.'

'What?' said Mandy. 'You mean those cards in shop windows show rooms and houses for renting?'

'Course they do,' Winston replied impatiently. 'Don't you ever use your eyes?'

'Oh shut up!' said Mandy. 'Come on, let's go to the pictures.' Together, the two of them left the café.

The next day, Mandy stopped by the shop window on her way to work, and looked to see if any rooms or flats were advertised. There were several cards showing places 'To Let,' but most of them seemed to be too expensive for Mandy. There were just a couple that seemed to be within the price that she could afford. One card said: 'To Let: bed-sitting room in Battersea. Suit single lady. £8.50 per week.' It gave a telephone number which Mandy copied down. She also copied another from a different card which said: 'To Let: one room in a house in Balham. Quiet lady preferred. £8.25 per week.'

During her tea-break she rang up about the house in Balham. She was a bit disappointed when she was told that the room had already been let. She was luckier with the other telephone number. The woman who answered the phone gave her the address of the room, and arranged to meet her outside the house at 7.30 that evening.

After she had finished on the telephone, she went back to work and sat down next to Sandra Carter. Mandy told Sandra that she was going to look at a bed-sitting room that evening.

'I wouldn't mind getting a place of my own,' said Sandra. 'I'm fed up with it at home: the way my stepfather bosses me around and keeps coming into my bedroom without knocking.'

'Perhaps we could get a place between us,' Mandy suggested. 'We get on all right together don't we?'

'Yeah, I wouldn't mind,' Sandra replied. 'We do get on O.K. and it wouldn't be any good trying to live with someone you don't get on with would it?'

At lunch-time, they went out to buy the local paper and looked through it to see if there were any flats to let. Most of them were too expensive. They had decided that the most they could afford was £19 per week between them. They telephoned a couple of accommodation agencies that specialised in finding people flats, but they were told that they would have to go to the agencies and register before they would be given any addresses. Mandy decided to go ahead and try to get the bed-sitter in Battersea.

She arrived at the address that the woman had given her just before half past seven. She was rather depressed to find that the house was in a seedy, run-down street just off the main road, and the continuous roar of the traffic could be heard quite plainly from where she was standing, just outside the house. The house itself looked dirty and uncared for. The bit of garden at the front was full of weeds and rubbish and the remains of an old bicycle.

At half past seven, a thin faced woman in a fur coat came up to the house and asked Mandy if she had come about the room. After asking Mandy her age and what work she did, she took her inside the house. The hall and the stairs were dusty and dirty. The woman opened the door of a room at the top of the stairs.

'This is the room,' she said in a hard, business-like voice.' 'It's £8.50 a week and you have a meter for gas and electricity that takes 10 pence a time. If you take the room, I shall want a month's rent in advance.'

Mandy's heart sank. The room was small and cramped, filled with cheap furniture that looked as if it came from a jumble sale. A small electric cooker was perched on a table near the sink and an ancient gas fire was the only source of heating. The room had a strange smell that reminded her of old men and dirty clothes. A single bed was by the window, which looked out onto the overgrown back garden and the wall of a warehouse. There was very little light coming into the room through the dusty windows. Mandy found it very depressing. She listened to a man coughing horribly in the next room.

The woman was speaking again. 'The toilets and the bathroom are just down the passage here and you share it with the other people who live upstairs. To have a bath, you put five pence in the meter.'

As she was speaking, a door at the end of the passage opened and a fat woman in a pink dressing gown waddled down to the bathroom. Her backside wobbled like a jelly as she walked.

'No thank you,' said Mandy to the woman. 'I think I'll stay at home for the time being.'

With a feeling of relief, Mandy left the woman and her house and caught the bus home. Sitting on the bus, she watched the rain begin to fall and she started to feel miserable and sorry for herself. She didn't want to live at home any longer, but neither did she want to live in a place like the one she had seen. What was she to do? Maybe she could get a place with Sandra. Perhaps something would turn up.

When she got home, she had an argument with her father about the clothes she was wearing. If only she could get away . . . .

Questions

1 Why did Mandy have a row with her mother?
2 What does Mandy do to help around the house?

3 What does Mandy's father get on to her about?
4 Why hasn't Mandy got a place of her own?
5 What sort of accommodation has Winston's brother got?
6 Why doesn't Mandy want to live in a place like Archie lives in?
7 Where are the best places to look for finding a place locally?
8 Where does Mandy see the rooms advertised the next morning?
9 How much rent would Mandy pay for four weeks in the room in Battersea and for four weeks in the room in Balham?
10 Why is Sandra fed up with living at home?
11 What kind of person does Sandra think it would be no good to live with?
12 What is the most that Mandy can afford to pay for rent?
13 What do accommodation agencies specialise in?
14 What would Mandy and Sandra have to do before the agencies would give them any addresses?
15 Why is Mandy depressed when she reaches the house?
16 What would Mandy have to pay for in addition to the rent if she accepted the room from the woman?
17 What other people in the house does Mandy notice?
18 What happens to Mandy when she gets home?

9 Looking for a Flat-Success!

The next day, Sandra asked Mandy, 'How did you get on with that room yesterday?'

'Ugh! It was really horrible,' Mandy said in disgust. 'It was just a tiny little room in a dirty old house. It looked a right old dump.'

'Look,' said Sandra, 'I've been thinking about that idea of getting a place between us. Do you honestly fancy it?'

'Why not?' Mandy replied. 'It would be good fun to share with someone else.'

'Well, let's try for a place together then,' said Sandra.

'It's a deal,' said Mandy, and they shook hands, laughing as they did so. For three weeks they tried the evening papers, the local papers, and the cards in the windows of every shop they passed. It wasn't nearly as easy as they thought it would be to find a place. Nearly always, the flats had been let by the time that they rang up, or they were too expensive. The two places that they got to before they were let were terrible.

One flat that they were offered was in Tooting. They found it from a notice board and took the bus over to the address they were given after they had finished work for the day. The man whom they met there took them down an alley between two houses around to the back of a house, then up a rickety old fire escape to two poky rooms that overlooked a busy main road. The rent he wanted for that was £18 per week, plus a ten per cent charge for electricity. Neither of the girls thought that the flat was worth taking.

They found the other place in an evening newspaper. When they arrived at the address that they were given, they were met by a very odd man who claimed to be the landlord.

He took them up three flights of stairs to the top of a big old house and showed them into one large room, with a sink and a cooker screened off by a piece of curtain in one corner. Two single beds were separated by a small bedside table.

'This is it,' said the man. 'It's seventeen pounds fifty a week, with four weeks paid in advance.'

'Where's the bathroom, Mr. uh . . .? You didn't say your name,' said Mandy.

'You don't need to know my name,' replied the man. 'The bathroom's just outside here. You share it with the other couple on this floor.'

'How long is the tenancy for?' asked Sandra.

'Don't know about that,' said the man. 'We've been having a bit of trouble with our tenants lately, so you won't get a rent book, we'll just give you a receipt.'

'You can keep the place then,' said Mandy, and grabbing Sandra's arm they left the man without saying another word.

When the two of them got outside, Mandy exploded. 'That man's just a crook!' she said. 'First of all he won't tell us his name, then he says we won't even get a rent book.'

'He wouldn't even say how long the tenancy was for,' said Sandra. 'Who cares about having a rent book?'

'That's the whole point,' Mandy answered. 'If he doesn't give us a rent book, we don't have any tenancy agreement. He can kick us out of there at any time he wants without giving us any notice at all.'

'What? You mean a rent book is like a tenancy agreement?' asked Sandra.

'More or less,' Mandy replied. 'Winston was telling me that if you have a rent book, the landlord can't kick you out without giving you proper notice. Once you have a rent book, he can't kick you out without a lot of fuss.'

They decided that they might have better luck if they went along to an accommodation agency, so on the following Saturday morning they went along to the agency that they had telephoned a few weeks earlier. When they got there, the man in charge took them into his office and asked them some questions.

'How much do you want to pay?' he asked them.

'No more than about nineteen pounds a week between us,' answered Mandy.

'Mmm,' said the man, 'well there aren't a lot of places that are available in that price bracket, and what there is goes very quickly.'

'Does that mean that there's nothing you can do for us?' asked Sandra.

The man smiled. 'No, not necessarily,' he said. 'We'll do what we can for you, but I'm afraid I can't promise anything. First of all though, I'd better explain how we operate. If you find a flat through us, you pay us a month's rent for using our services, and in return we do everything we can to find you a place.'

'What, pay you a month's rent on top of what we pay the landlord?' Mandy asked in disbelief.

'That's right,' said the man. 'Actually, it's four weeks' rent that we charge. Are you interested? I should add that if we don't find you anything, we don't charge you anything.'

'I don't know,' said Mandy. 'We'll have to talk it over first.'

Mandy and Sandra left the agency and went to have a cup of coffee and talk things over in a café. The café was crowded, so they sat down next to an old lady who was reading a paper, and started to discuss what the man in the agency had said.

'We could never afford the price they want us to pay for finding us a flat,' said Sandra. 'We just haven't got enough to pay the agency four weeks' rent, *and* pay a month's rent in advance.'

'I never thought it would be this difficult,' sighed Mandy. 'All we want is a little place of our own, and everyone wants to charge us the moon. I'm so fed up with living at home, I could cry.'

They sat in silence, looking into their coffee cups. Sandra began to sniff back the tears of frustration that were trying to come out of her. Suddenly the old lady sitting next to them spoke.

'Excuse me,' she said, 'but I couldn't help overhearing your conversation. What kind of a place is it that you're looking for?'

The two girls looked at her. She was aged about sixty, with silver hair and a lined face, but she was quite well-dressed, and she looked clever and alert.

'Well,' said Mandy, 'just a place of our own. A flat or something that we could share between the two of us.'

'And how much could you pay?' asked the woman.

'About nineteen pounds a week between us,' Mandy replied. 'Do you know of anywhere then?'

The woman smiled at them. 'As a matter of fact, I do know of somewhere, but first of all, I would like to ask you one or two questions. Do you have regular jobs?'

'Oh! yes,' said Sandra eagerly. 'We've both been working at the same place for the last ten months.'

'So your employer would be prepared to vouch for your reliability?' the woman asked.

'Yes. Definitely,' said Mandy. 'There'd be no problem there.'

'And what kind of work do you do?' asked the woman.

'We work at Community Industry, doing sewing and needlework and stuff,' Mandy answered. 'We could get references and that.'

'Good,' said the woman, smiling at them. 'As a matter of fact, I was just on my way to the accommodation agency down the road to tell them that one of my tenants has just quit his flat, and I was looking for two girls to take it over. Girls look after a place so much better than men, and they make less noise. Now it looks as if I've saved myself the trouble. Would you like to come and have a look at it? It's only just around the corner.'

Mandy and Sandra looked at each other. They could hardly believe their ears.

'Do you mean it?' asked Mandy. 'Have you really got a place?'

'Yes, of course,' the woman laughed. 'Come on, I'll show you it now while I'm down here.'

The three of them left the café and walked down some side streets until they came to a large semi-detached house in a quiet road that was lined with trees. The woman led them into the house and up some stairs to the first floor. Then she opened a door and led them into a large room that looked out over the street. The room needed a bit of tidying up, but it was nicely furnished and painted a cool, clean blue.

'This is half of it,' said the woman. She opened a door that led out of the room into a small kitchenette with a gas cooker that needed a clean, and some built-in cupboards that didn't. From the kitchen, a door opened into another room like the first one, though it was rather badly in need of a coat of paint. The two girls walked around it, looking at the chest of drawers and the wardrobe, and the double bed in one corner.

'I can always get another bed for the other room,' she said. 'Are you interested?'

'How much is it?' asked Mandy, trembling inside that it would be too much.

'I don't believe in charging excess rent,' said the woman. 'Young people find it hard enough to get along these days as it is. You can have the place for sixteen pounds fifty a week.'

'Oh! That's marvellous!' Sandra burst out. 'Let's take it!'

'Yeah, that's great!' said Mandy. 'Can we really have it?'

'Yes, providing that you can supply me with references.' The woman smiled at them. 'Of course, you pay your own gas and electricity, and you share the bathroom and toilets with the other people on this floor, but if you want the flat, I'll keep it for you. That's a promise. My name is Mrs. Moss, by the way.' She stretched out her hand, and the two girls introduced themselves.

When the two of them moved in a week later, the other room had been painted up, and once they had filled the rooms with their own things and put up their favourite posters, the flat looked quite homely.

'Funny, isn't it?' said Sandra. 'After all that worrying, something just falls in your lap.'

'Visiting that agency wasn't such a bad idea after all,' Mandy answered, warming her legs by the hissing gas fire.

Questions

1 Where is the first flat that Mandy and Sandra are offered?
2 Where do they see the flat advertised?
3 Where else do they look to see flats advertised?
4 What is the first flat like?
5 How much is 10% of the rent for the first flat?
6 Where do they see the second flat advertised?
7 How much money does the landlord want in advance?
8 Why is Mandy so concerned about getting a rent book off the landlord?
9 What else is suspicious about the landlord?
10 If the accommodation agency had found them a flat which charged rent of £17.50 per week, how much would they have to pay the agency?
11 Why do Mandy and Sandra leave the agency?
12 If the agency found them a flat which charged rent of £18.00 per week, and they had to pay four weeks' rent in advance, how much would they have to pay out altogether?
13 What questions does the old lady ask the girls?
14 What kind of street is the old lady's flat in?
15 How many rooms does the flat have, including the kitchenette?
16 What other expenses will the girls have to pay, besides the rent?
17 What must Mandy and Sandra supply to Mrs. Moss if they are to get the flat?

* * *

A If you wanted a flat, how would you set about finding one?
B If you were asked to give references to a landlord, what kind of people would you give?
C What are the advantages and disadvantages of living away from home?

10 Job Prospects: Attitudes and Interviews

Tommy Brown had applied for a job as a Trainee Painter with Hobbs and Son Limited just over a week before he was invited to attend an interview. He received a letter in the morning post, and the interview was set for the following day. He spent most of the day before his interview discussing with his workmates at Community Industry how he might best get the job. Everyone was giving him advice, but some of it seemed a bit contradictory.

His cousin Jimmy, for instance, told him to dress casually, and to appear eager to get the job. 'You don't want to get all dressed up as if you were going to a wedding,' said Jimmy. 'You should dress like you were ready to start work right away. Blimey! You're only going for a job as a flippin' painter, not a bank manager. Mind you,' he continued, 'you should make it obvious that you're dead keen to get the job. You know, like, "I really do want to be a painter with 'Obbs and Son. It's the ambition of me life. I'll work 'til me fingers drop off, then I'll paint with me feet Guv'nor. Honest I will . . ." Know what I mean, Tom?' Jimmy grinned at him.

'Do you reckon that that's the best way of gettin' the job then?' asked Tommy, a bit doubtfully.

'Course it is,' said Jimmy. 'You got to chance yer luck, ain't you?'

'Well, I don't think that's the way at all,' interrupted Winston Lewis, who had been listening to the conversation. 'You should wear your smartest clothes to an interview. That's what I was always told. The other thing I was told is that you shouldn't make yourself seem so eager to get the job that the man who's interviewing you thinks he's doing you a favour. Play it a bit cool.'

'That must be why you never got that other job that you

went after,' said Jimmy, grinning at him. 'Who ever heard of going to an interview and acting as if you didn't want the job?'

'That's not what I'm saying,' replied Winston quickly. 'What I'm saying is that you shouldn't seem so keen to get the job that you're almost begging for it.'

'Who's talking about begging for a job?' Russell Bannerman inquired. He was another of the young men working at Community Industry. 'You must be mad, begging for a job. What's wrong with it here?'

'No one's begging for a job,' replied Tommy. 'I've got an interview tomorrow for a painting job, that's all.'

'What, working on a site?' asked Russell.

'Yeah, I suppose so,' answered Tommy.

'Get on. You're daft you. You wouldn't catch me on a site,' said Russell. 'That's dirty work that is. And I bet you won't get paid much. Not as much as you get here.'

'Well, what are you going to do then?' Winston jeered at him. 'You can't stop here forever, making your little speakers.'

'I'm going to get a job in a clothes shop,' Russell replied, 'where I can stay clean and make plenty of money.'

'Oh yeah?' sneered Tommy. 'You mean where you can grease up to the customers and brown-nose round the boss don't you? Anyway,' he continued, 'you need "O" levels for that.'

'No you don't,' replied Russell. 'A mate of mine reckons I could get in O.K. He works in a clothes shop, and you should see the clothes he's got. And he's got a motor.'

'Big deal,' said Tommy, turning away from Russell, who returned to chipping away at the speaker box he was making.

'Get on, Russell,' jeered Winston. 'You got no chance. I bet you end up back on the dole when you leave here.'

Russell looked up from his work and replied, 'Well at least it'll be better than working me guts out in the freezing cold, stuck on a moody site somewhere.'

'He gets right up my nose, that bloke,' said Tommy, as

the three of them moved away from Russell. 'What does he know anyway? No one asked him to butt in.'

'Aw, forget him,' Jimmy answered. 'He's all mouth and trousers. How're you going to handle it tomorrow then?'

'I dunno,' said Tommy. 'I think I'll go and ask Ed.'

Ed's advice to Tommy was straightforward and simple. 'Don't dress up, and don't dress down,' he said. 'It's O.K. for you to wear your casual clothes, but make sure you look smart rather than scruffy. The way you present yourself at an interview reflects on the way you'll present your work. So if you look scruffy and slipshod at an interview, the chances are that your work will turn out to be equally scruffy. You can be relaxed, without being untidy.'

'Yeah. I think that makes sense,' replied Tommy. 'What about this business of showing them how keen I am to get the job?'

'Well,' said Ed thoughtfully, 'you don't want to give them so much bull that they think that you're just shooting them a line. Be sincere. If you want the job, let them know it, and if they want you, they'll take you. The actual selection of the bloke they want for the job is up to them. There's only so much that you can do.'

'Thanks, Ed,' said Tommy as he left the office.

'Best of luck, Tommy,' said Ed.

Questions

1 What sort of job had Tommy applied for?
2 Where was Tommy working?
3 How does Jimmy think that Tommy should dress for his interview?
4 Do you think Jimmy's advice is good? Why?
5 How does Winston think that Tommy should dress for his interview?
6 Do you think that Winston's advice is good? Why?

7 What is Russell's attitude towards working on a site?
8 What sort of a job does Russell want?
9 Do you think that Russell has a good attitude towards work? Why?
10 What does Russell make at work?
11 What does Tommy say that Russell needs to be able to work in a shop?
12 What kind of advice does Ed give Tommy?
13 How does Ed tell Tommy that he should behave towards his interviewers?
14 What does Ed tell Tommy about the way that people present themselves at an interview?
15 Whose advice do you think that Tommy is most likely to take?

✳   ✳   ✳

Points for discussion

A How do you think that you should dress for an interview?
B How do you think that you should behave at an interview?
C For what reasons do bank managers dress differently to painters and tradesmen?

11 On Site: Attitudes to Work

'I'm getting fed up with this,' Anthony Roach remarked to his workmate Tommy Brown.

'Fed up with what?' asked Tommy.

'Fed up with that nutter Harvey Warren,' Anthony replied. 'He's driving me up the wall, with his messing about and making a row.'

The two of them were hard at work, painting up the inside of a terraced house so that it would be fit for someone to live in. Tommy and Anthony were doing the ground floor, and Harvey Warren and Russell Bannerman were supposed to be doing the top floor. From the noise that they were making however, it didn't sound as if much work was getting done up there. It sounded more like they were having a party! What made it worse for the two working downstairs was the fact that every now and again one of them would creep downstairs and throw a piece of wood or a cup of water at the two who were trying to work.

'You just want to ignore him,' Tommy advised his friend. 'Just leave them alone and get on with our own work.'

When eleven o'clock arrived, Tommy and Anthony went out onto the front porch to eat their sandwiches. As they were sitting down in the sunshine, they were joined by the two youths from upstairs.

'How are you two creeps getting on then?' Russell Bannerman asked them with a sneer.

'A bloody sight better than you two layabouts,' Tommy answered. 'I bet you haven't even got the room stripped yet.'

'I wouldn't mind getting that stripped,' said Harvey Warren, looking across the road at a young woman who was emptying some rubbish into a dustbin.

'Get on,' jeered Russell, 'you wouldn't know where to start!'

'Oh no?' said Harvey. 'Since when were you such a great Casanova then?'

'I bet you wouldn't dare to go over and slap her on the bum then,' Russell said.

'How much do you want to bet?' Harvey asked him.

'Bet you ten pence.'

Harvey jumped up and ran swiftly across the road. He came up behind the young woman and tapped her lightly on the backside, before beating a hasty retreat back to join his friends. He did not see the woman turn around and glare fiercely at him before vanishing back into her house.

'Pay up then,' Harvey ordered Russell.

'No chance!' Russell jeered. 'You never even touched her.'

'I did. You saw me do it,' Harvey complained.

'I was looking the other way,' said Russell.

'That's the last time I trust you then,' Harvey replied bitterly.

'Ahhh! I think I'm going to cry,' Russell sneered sarcastically.

'You act like little kids at school, you lot,' said Tommy in disgust. He got up and went back inside. Anthony followed him.

Russell nudged his mate and whispered to him. Then he picked up a lump of wood and crept up to the door of the room where the other two were working. He threw the wood into the room as hard as he could. This was immediately followed by a scream of pain. Russell turned to grin at his mate, but found that Harvey wasn't looking at him. Harvey was looking towards a burly looking young man who was coming across the road, tucking his shirt into his trousers and looking extremely angry. He walked straight up to Harvey, and grabbed him by his shirt front.

'What's the big idea then, you little creep?' he asked Harvey.

'What? What? I don't know what you're talking about. Let go of me!' Harvey bleated. Russell ducked back into the house only to find himself grabbed around the neck by a very annoyed Tommy Brown.

'You stupid bastard,' hissed Tommy into his ear as he choked him.

'Get off!' gasped Russell. 'You're choking me!'

A cry of pain and fear came from the front of the house, where Harvey had just received a butt in the face from the husband of the woman he'd slapped on the backside.

'That wood went straight into Tony's eye, you stupid, mindless idiot!'

'Let go of my neck,' choked Russell. 'I'll hammer you if you don't.'

'Try it,' said Tommy, releasing him and standing up to him with his fists bared.

Russell aimed a punch at Tommy which missed him, then felt his nose explode as Tommy's fist connected with it. He fell over as another punch from Tommy caught him in the eye.

Tommy stood over him. 'Have you had enough?' he asked the bleeding youth on the floor.

Russell felt all the fight go out of him as he realised that Tommy was a much better fighter than he was, and that to continue would only result in more pain for himself.

'All right Brown,' he muttered sullenly, 'you win.'

The man came in from the front door, dragging Harvey Warren by the scruff of his dirty shirt. Harvey's nose was bleeding and so was his mouth, where the man had knocked three of his front teeth out.

'Who's in charge here?' the man asked.

'He's away at the moment,' replied Tommy.

'You ought to be ashamed of yourselves, attacking defenceless women,' said the man.

'It was nothing to do with me and my mate,' said Tommy evenly. He indicated Russell, who was standing in a corner brushing himself off. 'This idiot dared him to do it. Then he nearly put my mate's eye out with a piece of wood.'

Anthony Roach came to the door of the hall in which they were standing, with his hand over one eye. Blood was oozing between his fingers.

The man kept hold of Harvey with one hand, and with the other he grabbed hold of Russell. 'Listen,' he said. 'You aren't at school now. You don't get sent to the head teacher if you annoy someone. You don't get told off for being rude or aggravating any more. You get your bloody head kicked in, or you get the sack, or you find yourself involved in a lot of aggravation. Understand?' He knocked their heads together with a crack that jarred their teeth.

Just then Ed, the supervisor came in.

'What's going on here then?' said Ed.

'Are you in charge of this lot then?' asked the man.

'Blimey!' said Ed. 'It looks like the Battle of Waterloo in here. What's been happening?'

'I asked if you were in charge here,' said the man.

'That's right,' said Ed. 'Who are you?'

'I'm the husband of the woman who this little creep assaulted,' replied the man, pushing Harvey forward. 'And this is the little toe-rag who encouraged him to do it.' He pulled Russell forward.

'What happened to Anthony's eye?' asked Ed.

Tommy spoke up! 'Russell threw a piece of wood at him,' he said.

'What's the idea of leaving a load of little maniacs like this in a place without supervision?' the man asked.

'They were supposed to be all right on their own for a bit,' said Ed. 'Obviously they're not.'

'You ought to be locked up, mate,' the man said to Ed. 'People have to live around here whilst these idiots are working here. Who do you work for?'

'Community Industry,' Ed replied.

'I've heard about that lot,' said the man. 'I'm going to write to the newspapers about this. It's a waste of taxpayer's money and a menace to the respectable people who these kids are working around. You'll hear more about this.' The man stormed out of the house.

There was a silence in the hall. Ed was breathing hard. Finally he spoke.

'Right Russell and Harvey, let's see what you've done so far today.'

Russell and Harvey looked at each other, then they walked up the stairs behind Ed. Tommy looked at Anthony's eye while they waited in the hall. It was swollen and the eyebrow was cut rather badly, but the eye itself was all right. 'The eye's O.K., but I think you'd better go down the hospital to get it stitched,' he told Anthony.

Ed came back down the stairs with the other two. Russell and Harvey walked out of the front door without saying a word. Ed was still breathing heavily.

'What's happening to those two then?' Tommy asked Ed.

'I've given them the boot. That's what,' Ed replied. 'Wasting time and messing about; stopping other people from getting on with their work, and annoying the local people where they're working. They've already had two written warnings about their work attitude, and now they've had it.'

'Good job too,' said Anthony. 'All they ever did was cause a load of aggravation.'

'Yeah,' said Ed. 'Well you'd better get down to the hospital to see about that eye. Will you go with him Tommy, and then report back to me in Battersea?'

'Sure,' said Tommy.

'See you later then,' said Ed, as he locked the door of the house where they were working, and Tommy and Anthony walked off through the sunshine towards the 'bus stop.

Questions

1 What was Anthony Roach getting fed up with?
2 What were the four of them supposed to be working at?
3 What is Tommy's advice to Anthony about the antics of the other two?
4 Why does Harvey go over and smack the woman's backside?
5 What does Tommy say about the way that Russell and Harvey act?
6 What does Russell do after Anthony and Tommy go back inside the house?
7 What is the burly man doing as he is coming across the road? Who is he?
8 How does the man attack Harvey?
9 Do you think that he was right to attack Harvey? Why?
10 Why does Tommy attack Russell?
11 Do you think he was right to attack Russell? Why?
12 What does the man do to Harvey's face?
13 What does the man say happens to people who annoy other people, once they have started work?
14 Do you agree with him? Why?
15 What does the man tell Ed that he is going to do?
16 What has Russell's messing about done to Anthony's eye?
17 What reasons does Ed give for sacking Russell and Harvey? Was he right?
18 What does Ed tell Anthony and Tommy to do?
19 Do you think that Ed was right to leave the four youths to work on their own? Why?

*   *   *

A What would you say the most important differences between being at work and being at school?
B In what ways does your attitude have to change, once you have left school, if you are to be successful at work?
C Do you think that people have a responsibility to behave themselves when they are working in a residential area?
D What kind of reasons would you think are a fair reason for being sacked from work?

12 The Interview

It was pouring with rain as Tommy Brown made his way to Clapham Junction Station. He cursed under his breath at the bad weather because he was going to be interviewed for a job over in Streatham Hill, and he was wearing his best trousers. There wasn't much hope of his looking smart when he was soaking wet! He pulled his cap down further and turned the collar of his jacket to the wind, and with his shoulders hunched against the rain he trudged into the station, mixing with the end of the rush-hour crowds.

After waiting for about ten minutes, he finally boarded the Beckenham train to Streatham Hill. He sat down in a corner of the carriage and watched the buildings roll past the windows. He felt damp and cold and a bit uneasy. He wanted this job, but he was not at all sure that he was going to get it. He only had two C.S.E. passes, and wasn't sure how much his experience at Community Industry would count in his favour. Still, he thought to himself, it wasn't the end of the world if he didn't get it. He still had another month at Community Industry before his year was up.

It had stopped raining by the time the train pulled in at Streatham Hill. There were only a few people about on the station as Tommy moved out into the High Road. The clock on the station wall showed a quarter to ten. He had fifteen minutes to get to Hobbs and Son's yard. Walking briskly, Tommy reached the yard in a few minutes. It was up a side street, just off the High Road. Tommy checked the address, then went back to the main street to comb his hair in a shop window and check that he looked presentable. As he stepped back from the window to admire his appearance – or moan at it – Tommy bumped into a grey-haired man who was walking past him.

'Sorry,' said Tommy.

'Not at all,' replied the man, taking a step backwards and smiling at him briefly before moving on and vanishing around a corner.

Tommy turned to face his reflection again. He looked all right. He hung about on the corner for a minute as he didn't want to arrive too early, then he walked down into the yard of Hobbs and Son and asked for the office. He was directed to a long, low building in the corner of the yard.

Tommy knocked on the door and went in. A man was hanging up his coat on a clothes stand. As Tommy closed the door, the man turned to face him. It was the man he had bumped into up on the corner.

'Good morning,' said the man.

'G' morning,' replied Tommy, standing awkwardly by the door.

'Do sit down,' said the man, indicating a chair in front of his desk. Tommy and the man sat down facing each other.

'What can I do for you?' asked the man.

'My name's Tommy Brown. I've come to be interviewed for the painting job,' said Tommy.

The man stood up and shook hands with Tommy. 'I'm Mr. Hobbs,' he said. 'My son will be here soon. Didn't I bump into you up in the High Road?'

Tommy grinned rather sheepishly. 'That's right,' he said. 'I was just making sure that I looked all right.'

'Good,' said Mr. Hobbs. 'I like to see a lad who takes care of his appearance.'

Tommy mumbled something and felt rather embarrassed.

The door opened behind him, and a smartly dressed young man walked in carrying a brief-case. 'Morning, Dad,' he said. 'Is this Mr. Brown?'

'Yes,' said Mr. Hobbs. 'Mr. Brown, this is my son Alan Hobbs.'

Tommy stood up and shook hands with Alan Hobbs. 'How do you do?' he said.

'Fine, thank you,' said Alan Hobbs. He moved over and sat down by the side of his father's desk, then opened his briefcase and took out some papers and a pen. He looked across at Tommy. 'Now Mr. Brown,' he said, 'you want to work with us as a Trainee Painter, do you?'

'Yes,' said Tommy. He didn't think that sounded very impressive, so he added, 'I want to learn to become a qualified painter.'

'What experience have you had of painting?' the older Mr. Hobbs asked him.

'Well, uh, I've been working at Community Industry as a painter for the last year,' said Tommy. He hesitated a moment, then added, 'I helped my Dad decorate the house last year as well.'

'What kind of painting at Community Industry?' said Mr. Hobbs. 'What sort of work have you been doing?'

'House painting mostly,' said Tommy. 'We've been doing up a lot of old houses over in Battersea lately. Painting up the insides and doing the outside woodwork.'

'Do you like that kind of work?' Mr. Hobbs asked him.

'Yes,' said Tommy. 'It's nice to see the houses after they've been done up. You feel that you've been working at something worthwhile.'

'Good,' said Mr. Hobbs. 'What do you want to ask Mr. Brown, Alan?'

Alan Hobbs looked at Tommy and said, 'If you had a wall twelve feet by twelve feet, and a tin of paint that could cover 72 square feet, how many tins would you need to cover the wall?'

Tommy felt his stomach turn over and his mind went blank. He thought to himself, 'That's that job down the pan.' Aloud he said, 'I'm afraid I don't know that.'

'Mmm,' said Mr. Hobbs, stroking the side of his nose and looking down.

'Well, at least you say so when you don't know something,' said Alan Hobbs. 'Do you know how to multiply?'

'Oh yes. I can do that all right,' Tommy replied, feeling a glimmer of hope that he might still get the job.

'You know for instance what twelve twelves are?' Alan Hobbs persisted.

'Uh' . . . said Tommy, his mind racing. He thought for a second and felt his face turning red. 'A hundred and forty four,' he blurted out.

'Right,' said Alan Hobbs. 'Did they teach you to work out square feet at school, or didn't they bother?'

Tommy thought that they probably had, but he'd forgotten it. He said, 'No, I don't think they did.' He paused for a moment, then felt forced to add, 'Or at least if they did, I've forgotten it.'

'Well, you'll have to learn it again if you come and work for us,' said Mr. Hobbs rather gruffly.

'That's fair enough,' said Tommy. 'I don't mind learning things I need to know. I wouldn't forget anything I needed to know in my work.' He felt that the interview was going against him, but he continued speaking, almost desperately. 'That's why I've applied for the job, see; so I can learn the trade properly; learn all the different things I need to know.' He stopped, feeling that he was talking too much. He felt like a smoke, but he reminded himself that it was rude to smoke in an interview. He was relieved to notice Mr. Hobbs nodding in approval.

'Yes, that seems reasonable,' said Mr. Hobbs. 'We've all got to start somewhere.'

'How many C.S.E.'s have you got?' Alan Hobbs asked him.

'I've got English and Woodwork,' Tommy replied. 'I would have got Art, but I was away when they had the exam.'

After a moment, Mr. Hobbs said, 'How much would you expect to earn if you started with us?'

'Uh . . . well . . . I don't know,' Tommy stammered. 'Whatever you think I'm worth.'

'Righto,' said Mr. Hobbs, 'we would start you at 75 pence an hour, and take it from there, see how you get on.'

'That would be fine,' said Tommy. He couldn't quite work out if that meant that he'd got the job. He did a quick calculation, working out that if he did 40 hours work a week, it would bring in more than he was getting at Community Industry, and he'd be learning a trade.

'Could you start on Monday?' Mr. Hobbs asked him.

Tommy felt his spirits lift. 'Yes, that wouldn't be any problem,' he said.

Mr. Hobbs looked at his son, then back at Tommy. 'All right Mr. Brown. That's all we want to ask you.'

'Does that mean that I've got the job then?' Tommy asked.

Mr. Hobbs smiled at him. 'No,' he said. 'It means that we haven't made our minds up.' He watched Tommy's face fall, then said kindly, 'If you wait outside for a minute, we can tell you now if you've got it. Usually we write to tell people if we want them or not.'

Tommy left the room, feeling rather foolish. He waited nervously for about two minutes, then the door of the office opened and he was called back in.

'Right,' Mr. Hobbs said, smiling at him, 'you can start on Monday morning. It's Tommy isn't it?'

'That's right.' Tommy smiled. 'Well, thank you very much.'

'Be in the yard at 8 o'clock sharp,' said Alan Hobbs, 'and don't forget your overalls.'

'Don't worry. I won't forget anything,' Tommy replied. He walked back up to the High Road. He wanted to jump into the air. At long last, he'd got the job he wanted!

Questions

1 Why did Tommy think that he wouldn't look smart for his interview?
2 How long did Tommy have to go before his time at Community Industry was up?

3 What time was it when Tommy reached Streatham Hill?
4 What time was Tommy's interview for?
5 Why did Tommy go back to the main street?
6 Who did Tommy bump into in the High Road?
7 Did Tommy's bumping into the man make a good or a bad impression? Why?
8 Where had Tommy been doing up houses?
9 Why does Tommy like doing up houses?
10 What is the area in square feet of a wall 12 feet by 12 feet?
11 If one tin of paint covered 72 square feet, how many tins would you need to cover the wall?
12 If you were asked a question that you could not answer at an interview, would you make a guess at the answer, or simply admit that you didn't know?
13 Why does Tommy say that he has applied for the job?
14 Why does Tommy not have a smoke in the interview?
15 How many C.S.E.'s does Tommy have?
16 If Tommy worked 40 hours a week at a rate of 75 pence an hour, how much would his gross wages be?
17 What is the difference between Mr. Hobbs asking Tommy, 'Could you start on Monday?' and asking him, 'Can you start on Monday?'
18 How did Mr. Hobbs normally tell people if they had been accepted for a job or not?

                    *   *   *

A Is it advisable to arrive (i) exactly on time for your interview, (ii) early for your interview, (iii) a bit late for your interview? Give your reasons.
B If you are asked a question, should you answer it (i) slowly and clearly, (ii) as quickly as possible, (iii) in great detail?
C Imagine you were asked for an interview for your ideal job. Describe what the job consists of, and describe your interview for it, imagining the kind of questions that you would be asked, and how you would reply to them.

13 Holiday Preparations

The rain pattered down on the window panes in the darkness outside Sandra Carter's room. The wind was blowing the rain in sheets against the glass, and both Sandra and her boyfriend, Tommy Brown, were glad to be sitting warm and safe inside the brightly lit room, rather than getting soaking wet and cold outside.

'Poor old Mandy and Winston,' said Sandra, 'I bet they wish they hadn't bothered going out now.' She snuggled up to Tommy who was lying at her side on the carpet by the fire.

'Well, I'm glad they went out,' Tommy replied. 'It's nice to be on our own once in a while.' He grinned at her.

Sandra grinned back at him. 'I know what you mean,' she said.

The two of them lay in silence by the hissing gas fire, listening to the sound of the falling rain gusting through the city streets.

'Tommy,' said Sandra, breaking the silence, 'why don't we go on holiday together this year?'

'Haven't got any money,' Tommy replied briefly.

'You have,' Sandra insisted. 'Now that you've got a proper job, you could easily save some money each week, and I could too, and we could go somewhere nice together.'

Tommy sat up. 'Now that you come to mention it,' he said, 'I suppose we could do that. I'm bound to be able to save something from my wages each week.'

'Course you are,' Sandra replied eagerly, and with what we could save together, we could go somewhere really nice, like Devon or Bournemouth.'

'Who wants to go to those dumps?' said Tommy contemptuously, getting up from the mat as he spoke. 'They're just full of old people who go there to retire.'

'That's not true,' said Sandra. 'We went to Newquay once, and it was full of young kids from the towns. There were loads of discos and clubs, and the beach was really smashing.'

'I'd like to go to Spain,' Tommy announced. 'I know this geezer who went there, and he said he had the best time of his life.'

'But we can't speak Spanish,' Sandra objected. 'How can we go there if we can't speak Spanish?'

'You don't have to speak Spanish, because they all speak English over there. You can even buy fish and chips there, my mate said.' Tommy continued, getting more excited, 'He said there were loads of discos over there, and that everything was really cheap, and it was always really boiling hot.'

A gust of rain rattled the glass of the window. Tommy looked towards the sound and pulled a face. 'If we go on holiday here, it will most likely rain all the time.'

'How much would a holiday in Spain cost then?' asked Sandra.

'I dunno,' Tommy replied, 'but I shouldn't think it could be all that expensive if old Ronny Scannell could afford it. He doesn't earn all that much.'

'I'll go to the travel agents tomorrow and find out,' said Sandra. 'If you come round tomorrow night, I'll get hold of a load of brochures, and we can work out what we can afford.'

'Fair enough,' replied Tommy. 'Why not?'

When he got round to the flat on the following evening, he found Winston and Mandy there, as well as Sandra. Sandra explained to him that she had got Mandy interested in the idea of the holiday, and that Mandy had in turn got Winston's interest. Tommy was a bit put out. He knew both Winston and Mandy well enough, but he had thought that the idea was for Sandra and him to go away by themselves. As the idea of going as a foursome sank in, however, he found that he quite liked the idea. They could probably have more fun together. What convinced him more than anything though, was the money aspect of going as four rather than two.

'Look,' said Sandra, 'if we go as four people together, we can get a ten-day holiday on the Costa Brava for just £350. That's including hotel rooms and air flight.'

'How much would that be between us then?' asked Tommy.

After working out how much each of them would pay, they started to work out how much they would need for food and spending money. They decided that they would need at least £3 a day each for food, on top of any spending money, if they took a holiday which did not include the price of meals at their hotel. They made up their minds to take their holiday in early September, because, Sandra explained, the price was cheaper then as it was the end of season and there weren't so many people about, and the weather was still warm. It was now the end of February, so they had about six months to save the money that they needed.

They looked at some other kinds of holidays. The 'package-deal' type holidays were the cheapest. This kind of holiday was sold as a 'package,' which included flight out and back; the price of hotel accommodation; and some, or all, of your meals.

'Here's one,' said Winston, looking up from his brochure. 'This one's for ten days in Marbella: food, flight, and hotel all included: £440 for four people.'

'That's more expensive than the one on the Costa Brava,' Tommy complained.

'Not really,' replied Winston, 'not if you bear in mind that all your meals are included.'

They worked out which was the cheaper of the two holidays, and found that Winston was right. The one with all the meals included would be cheaper, but they didn't know if they wanted it.

'It would mean that we'd have to keep going back to the hotel all the time,' Sandra complained.

'Yeah,' Mandy agreed. 'We couldn't have a proper day out by ourselves, and we'd always be tied to hotel meal times.'

'I'll tell you what I think,' said Tommy. 'I think it would be better to just get a place with bed and breakfast. We can always buy food from the shops for lunch, and we can have a proper meal in the evenings in a café or something.'

Sandra wasn't so sure. 'Look at this here,' she said. 'There's one here that's got ten days in a hotel in Rosas, with breakfast and evening meal, £410.00 for four people.'

'This one's better,' said Mandy. 'Ten days in a hotel in Torremolinos with bed and breakfast: £385.00 for four people, including flight out and back with British Airways.'

'That sounds like good value,' said Tommy. 'Sounds like just what we want. Have breakfast, then down to the beach; have a few sandwiches or something for lunch; afternoon by the beach, then a meal in a local café, followed by a night in the disco. Magic.'

'Yeah, that sounds great,' said Winston enthusiastically. 'Do you really think we can do it?'

'The one with just bed and breakfast is definitely the cheapest,' said Sandra, 'but how much money will we need?'

They were silent for a while until Tommy said thoughtfully, 'I think we could do it on about five quid a day spending money.'

'That would be loads,' said Mandy. 'I wouldn't think we'd need as much as all that.'

'Well, let's do a few sums,' Sandra said, 'and work out how much we can afford to save.'

After they had worked out a few figures of how much they needed to save each month, they were delighted.

'We can do it easily,' said Tommy. 'All we need to do is cut down on going out for a couple of nights a week.'

'Great!' Winston said. 'Shall we shake on it?'

They all shook hands on the agreement, then Winston and Tommy left.

Questions

1 Where are the first places that Sandra suggests for a holiday?
2 Why doesn't Tommy want to go there?
3 What is Sandra's objection to going to Spain?
4 Where does Sandra go to find out about holidays abroad?
5 How much would they each have to pay towards the holiday for four on the Costa Brava?
6 How much extra would each of them need for food over the ten-day period?
7 Including the cost of extra money for food, how much would the holiday on the Costa Brava come to, not counting any other spending money?
8 How much would each one of them have to pay to make up this amount?
9 How much would each of them have to pay to make up the cost of the holiday in Marbella?
10 Approximately how much would each of them have to save each month to pay for the holiday in Marbella?
11 How much would each of them have to pay to make up the cost of the holiday in Rosas?
12 Approximately how much would each of them have to save each month to pay for the holiday in Rosas?
13 How much would each of them have to pay to make up the cost of the holiday in Torremolinos?
14 Approximately how much would each of them have to save each month to pay for the holiday in Torremolinos?
15 How much spending money would each of them need altogether?
16 Including spending money and the cost of the package holiday, how much would each of them need to save for the holiday in Torremolinos?
17 How much would each of them have to save each week to save this amount each month?
18 How does Tommy suggest that they can save the money?

14 A Narrow Escape

Winston Lewis and his girlfriend Mandy Sloane were walking home from a late-night session at 'Clouds,' a discotheque in Brixton. It was almost two o'clock in the morning, and both of them were feeling very tired. There were very few people about on the streets, and only the occasional car lit them up briefly with its headlights as they purred past through the almost sleeping town. Winston and Mandy moved up past a line of shop fronts, heading towards Acre Lane.

'Hey, look at that!' said Winston suddenly, pointing into a shop doorway. Mandy turned and looked in the direction that Winston was pointing. The door leading into a clothes shop was ajar. There were no lights on in the shop, and the coast seemed clear for anyone who wanted to steal as many clothes as they wanted!

Mandy tugged at Winston's arm. 'Come on Winston,' she said. 'We don't want to start messing around and getting in trouble with the Law. Let's get on home now, quickly.'

'Just hold on a minute,' Winston replied. 'Be cool. I'm just going to take a look at what's happening in there.' He let go of Mandy's arm, and moved into the shadows of the alcove leading to the shop doorway. He gently pushed the door wide open, then he vanished inside the darkened shop.

Mandy stood on the street outside feeling angry and scared. She spoke softly into the darkness. 'Winston! Come back here now and we get home before we get in trouble.' There was no reply. 'I'm going home by myself then,' she said angrily. Then suddenly she spoke in a voice that was hoarse with fear. 'Quick!' she said. 'There's someone coming!' Two men were walking down the street towards where Mandy stood waiting on the pavement outside the shop!

In a moment Winston appeared in the doorway of the shop. He was holding a leather coat in his hand. 'Who is it?' he whispered.

'Two men come. Let's go now. Leave that thing,' she pleaded.

At that moment they heard the sound of a police siren wailing in the distance. The noise seemed to bring Winston to his senses. He dropped the coat onto the floor of the alcove and moved out to join Mandy in the street, closing the door of the shop behind him as he came away. The two of them moved off quickly, putting as much distance as possible between them and the shop. The leather coat was left lying on the floor in the shadows.

Behind them, the two men walked up to the shop doorway and looked in as they passed. Seeing something lying in the shadows, one of the men walked in and picked it up, then the two of them walked on, following Winston and Mandy at a distance of about a hundred yards.

Winston and Mandy turned the corner into Acre Lane and saw a police car coming towards them! Winston felt his stomach turn and his mouth go dry as it slowed down and pulled in just in front of them.

One of the policemen in the car wound the window down. 'Where are you two off to then?' he asked.

'We're just on our way home, officer,' replied Mandy quickly.

'Where's that then?' said the policeman.

'What's that to you?' asked Winston. 'We haven't done anything wrong.'

A voice came through on the police radio, and the other policeman said to his companion, 'Come on. There's been a break in at a clothes shop just round the corner.'

'Did you see anything?' the first policeman asked Winston.

'I haven't seen anything happening. We've just come out of a disco,' Winston told him.

The policeman looked at him carefully, taking in his casual and obviously well-worn clothing, and noting the fact that neither of them was carrying anything that could be used to carry stolen clothes.

'All right,' he told them. 'Get on your way then.'

Winston and Mandy walked away quickly, and as they looked back, they saw the police car pull up by the two men with the coat just as they came around the corner into Acre Lane. Winston pulled Mandy into an alleyway, and they ran through a maze of back streets for what seemed to her like ages. Coming out into a main street, she was surprised to find herself just a little way from her flat.

She was still panting as she unlocked the front door. 'That was one narrow escape Mister Man,' she told Winston. 'I hope you'll listen to me next time.'

Winston too was out of breath, as he answered, 'Yes. For sure. That could have been some very bad news.'

The two of them clambered up the stairs to the flat. Mandy's flatmate Sandra was away for the week-end, so they had the place to themselves.

'Safe and sound and home at last!' said Mandy as she opened the door of the flat.

'Home, sweet home,' Winston said, grinning at her.

Mandy collapsed onto the sofa. 'Blimey!' she said. 'I'm really shattered.'

'Yeah,' Winston agreed as he sat down beside her.

Winston was the first to notice something was wrong.

'Here, Mandy,' he said, 'where's the telly?'

Mandy looked around her. 'Oh what!' she said in disbelief. 'Where's the radio and the tape-recorder? Winston! We've been burgled!'

Winston rose to his feet. 'I suppose I'd better get the cops,' he said.

Questions

1 At what time were Winston and Mandy walking home?
2 What did Winston point at that caused him and Mandy to stop?
3 What did Mandy say to Winston when she saw what he was pointing at?
4 What would you do if you saw an open shop-doorway at night?
5 Where did Winston go when he let go of Mandy's arm?
6 What did Mandy threaten to do when Winston was away from her?
7 Who did Mandy see coming towards them as she waited by the shop?
8 What did the noise of the police siren do to Winston?
9 What questions does the policeman ask Winston?
10 What happens to the leather coat that Winston leaves behind?
11 Why do the police not associate Winston with the break-in?
12 Who do the police stop next, after leaving Winston and Mandy?
13 Why do Winston and Mandy hide and go home by the back streets?
14 What do you think that the two men would have told the police?
15 What do you think would have happened if Winston had been carrying the leather coat when he was stopped by the police?
16 Do you think that the police were right to stop Winston and Mandy at all?
17 Name some of the things that are missing from the flat.
18 What does Winston decide to do when he realises that the flat has been burgled?

*   *   *

A If you were one of the policemen who stopped Winston and Mandy, and then the two men, what would you think had happened, regarding who was responsible for stealing the coat?
B Write a story describing what happened to the two men after they were stopped by the police.
C Is there always a definite right and wrong in cases of crime? What would you do if you saw a leather coat lying in a shop-doorway late at night? How would you feel if you were convicted for stealing it? Would you blame the police?
D Can you think of any other examples of crimes which the police find difficult to sort out, regarding guilt and innocence? Give examples.

15 Incident at the Youth Club

Winston Lewis and his girlfriend Mandy Sloane were on their way down to the youth club at Clapham. They hadn't visited the club before, but they'd heard from a friend of theirs that it was quite a good place, with a disco and a coffee bar, as well as table tennis and stuff like that. It was just starting to rain as they reached the club, and Winston was glad that they hadn't got caught in the storm that he felt was coming, as he'd got his new raincoat on! They walked up to the doors of the club and went in.

Two youths were sitting at a table with a book on it and they looked up as Winston and Mandy came in through the door. They scowled at him.

'What do you want?' one of them said to him. He was an ugly-looking character, with a pale, spotty face and a fluff of down on his top lip.

'We come to the club, what do you think we want?' Winston replied. He was rather upset by the rude way in which he had been greeted. He didn't intend taking any lip from anyone just because he hadn't been to a place before.

'You a member?' asked the other youth at the door, a youth with a swarthy face and a leather jacket.

'No,' replied Winston.

'Well you can't come in then,' said the spotty youth with a sneer.

'What do you mean, we can't come in?' Winston asked.

'Only members allowed in here, mate,' said the youth.

'Well how do we join then?' Mandy asked him.

'You have to be proposed by two other members, and pay fifty pence each,' said the swarthy-faced youth.

'We weren't told about that,' Winston complained. 'My

mate was down here last night, and he didn't pay anything.'

'Ah,' said the spotty faced one, 'well perhaps he had a mate down here to sign him in.'

'Who runs this place?' asked Winston. 'I thought it was supposed to be a club for the kids that live around here.'

'We're the kids what live round here,' said the youth with the leather jacket. 'We're the committee what runs the club, and we don't want a load of rubbish coming over from Brixton and trying to take it over. Get the picture, Sambo?'

'Who are you calling Sambo?' Winston replied angrily. 'You bloodclot honky raas!'

The two youths walked around the table and stood in front of Winston and Mandy.

'Time for you to push off chum, before you get hurt,' said the one with the spotty face.

'Come on, Winston,' said Mandy. 'We don't want to go in there anyway. Leave them to their stupid youth club.'

'Yeah,' said the one with the spotty face, 'leave us to our club and push off back to Brixton, and when the National Front comes to power, you can push off back to Africa.'

'Listen bumfluff,' said Winston, 'I ain't been to Africa yet, and I don't intend going anywhere just because some little pussy like you thinks he's a big man. If you want to call me names, just step outside one at a time, and we'll see who's going to push who around here.' Winston was really furious, particularly that they should have spoken to him like this in front of Mandy. He felt his pulse racing and his mouth was dry, but he was determined not to back down in front of these two racist bullies, even if it meant getting his head kicked in.

'Oh come on, Winston,' Mandy begged at his side, 'let's get out of here before something happens. You can't afford to get in trouble with the police. Let's go!'

'You keep out of this, Mandy,' said Winston. 'This is between me and these two cruts.'

Suddenly Winston felt himself grabbed by the back of his coat, and he was pulled outside. Mandy started shouting at whoever it was who had hold of him to let him go. It didn't seem to have any effect, Winston noted. He felt a wave of anger washing over him, and he turned around as far as he could, lashing out at whoever was holding him. It was with satisfaction that he felt his fist connect with bone. The hand released his collar, and he turned to face the man who grabbed him. It was a stocky man with a crew cut and an old army combat jacket on. Winston hit him again, and he went reeling backwards. The rain was falling hard now, and Winston felt it splashing onto his face. Then a light exploded in his head, and he fell forwards onto the wet pavement. . . .

He had a terrible headache and his neck felt broken when he woke up. Mandy was sitting beside him crying, and it was still raining. They were in a side road just past the railway bridge.

'How did we get here?' Winston asked thickly.

'They put us into a van,' Mandy replied. 'Oh, Winston! Are you all right? This is a terrible thing to happen. Are you all right? I thought they'd killed you.'

'Don't worry. I'm all right,' Winston moaned. He wished that he felt it as he said it. In fact he felt awful. 'Did they give me a kicking?' he asked.

'All three of them, after you went down,' said Mandy tearfully. 'I tried to stop them, but they just pushed me out of the way. It was horrible. They just kept on and on. I thought they were never going to stop.'

Winston struggled to his feet with his head reeling. The street lights seemed blindingly bright, but the rain on his face felt refreshingly cool. He had no idea what was the best thing he could do. He wanted revenge, but he didn't want to get his mates involved in a gang war. He staggered into the main road, and leaned against the wall of the bridge trying to clear his head. A police car pulled up alongside of him. The window of the car was wound down and a man looked out. The door of the car opened and a policeman got out and walked over to Winston.

'What's happening here then?' the policeman asked.

'Nothing,' said Winston. He didn't trust policemen. Too many of his friends had told him nasty tales about the police for him to trust them.

'Someone's given you a good hiding, sunshine. What did they do it for?' the policeman asked. He had a soft, pleasant voice and an easy manner.

'Ask them,' Winston replied. He felt a burning anger inside him, and was sure that the police weren't about to start helping him to get back at his enemies. The other policeman got out of the car and joined his mate. 'What's happening?' he asked.

Mandy suddenly blurted out at his side, 'It was those boys from that youth club up the road. They set on Winston and gave him a beating because he was black, and they told him to go back to Africa.'

The two policemen looked at one another. 'Did they mention the National Front?' the soft-voiced policeman asked.

'Yeah,' said Winston. 'Why? Are you members?'

'Don't be funny, kid,' said the second policeman. 'We're here to help you, and to uphold the law. If you've been beaten up, that's against the law. If you've been beaten because you're black, that's against the law too. Tell us who they were, and we'll pick them up. You'll have to help us though,' he added.

'Oh yeah?' said Winston.

'Did one of them have a crew-cut and an army jacket?' asked the soft-voiced policeman.

'That's right,' said Mandy. 'There was another one too, with a spotty face.'

'Baker and Cox,' said the second policeman to his mate. 'They've been at it again.'

'Listen, son,' said the soft-voiced one, 'the kids who did you over have been getting away with it for too long because no one will identify them for us. They're putting a nasty little gang together in that club. We're pretty sure it was them that put poor old Soap in hospital. Why don't you help us nail them?'

Winston remembered poor old Soap. His real name was Montgomery Green, but everyone called him Soap because he hardly ever washed. He'd been put in hospital a couple of weeks before by a bunch of kids, but no one knew who they were.

'I think you ought to help them, Winston,' said Mandy at his side.

'Soap's got a fractured skull and five broken ribs. You look like you've got a few scrapes and bruises yourself. Are you going to let them get away with it?'

Winston didn't answer. He couldn't decide what to do.

'Ah, leave the silly sod to get on with it,' the second policeman said. 'He deserves everything he gets if he's going just to forget it.'

Winston made his decision. 'All right,' he said, 'I'll take you to them.'

'Jump in then,' said the soft-voiced policeman moving towards the Panda car.

Winston and Mandy got into the car and directed the policeman towards the youth club. When they got to the club, the two youths who had stopped Winston were still on the door.

'That's two of them,' said Winston, pointing them out to the policemen.

'Good,' said the policeman with satisfaction. 'Baker's one of them. Do you know the other?' he asked his mate.

'No,' said the soft-voiced one, 'I don't think I've seen him before.'

As they were walking towards the door of the club, Winston saw the one in the army jacket who had grabbed him walking up to the other two. He said something to the other two, and they laughed. They stopped laughing when Winston and Mandy walked in with the two policemen.

'That's all three of them,' said Winston.

'What are you talking about?' said the one with the spotty face. 'I ain't never seen you before.'

The soft-voiced policeman said something softly into his radio, then he approached the three of them around the table.

'Been having a bit of fun have you lads?' he asked them.

The one in the army jacket grinned at him. 'It depends what you mean by a bit of fun,' he said.

'Well,' said the second policeman, 'let's start with assault and battery and actual bodily harm. That sounds like good fun.'

The grin vanished from the youth's face. 'Here,' he said, 'you're not going to believe that creep are you? We never touched him.'

'It looks like it,' the policeman replied. He went on, 'Let's have your names.'

The three of them grumbled and moaned, but gave the police their names and addresses just the same. Then the policeman with the soft voice said that he was charging them, and cautioned them over what they said. Eventually another police car arrived and the three of them got into it. Winston and Mandy drove down to the police station with the two policemen, and when they got there, they found a fight going on in front of the desk. It turned out that the three youths had been carrying knives, and when they were searched, they tried to run off. After they had been quietened down, Winston and Mandy made their statements, then the policemen drove them to Brixton.

'What will happen to them?' Winston asked the policemen as they drove back home.

'Oh, they're in bad trouble now,' was the reply. 'On top of what they did to you, they'll be charged with assaulting the police, carrying offensive weapons. They'll spend the night in the cells, and go to prison for a few months, I should think.' Winston grinned to himself. It hadn't been such a bad idea to get the police in after all.

Questions

1 Why wasn't Winston allowed in the club?
2 How do you become a member of the club?
3 Who runs the club?
4 How do the club members insult Winston?
5 How does Winston insult them back?
6 What does Mandy want Winston to do when he is being insulted?
7 What do you think Winston should have done?
8 Describe the appearance of the man whom Winston hits.
9 Where does Winston wake up after he is knocked out?
10 What does Mandy tell Winston that the three club members did to him?
11 Why didn't Winston trust policemen?
12 Do you think he is right not to trust them?
13 What does the policeman tell Winston that the job of the police is?
14 Do you think that the policeman is speaking the truth about this? Why?
15 Who was 'Soap,' and what happened to him?
16 Do the policemen know the people who beat Winston up?
17 What charges do the police mention to the club members?
18 How do the three club members get into worse trouble at the police station?

*   *   *

A Have you ever had any experience of racial prejudice? Describe any of them.
B Have you ever called upon the police for assistance? Did you find them helpful or not? Describe any such experience.
C Have you ever been in trouble with the police? Describe such an experience.
D Do you think that a person's colour can tell you much about the kind of person that he or she is? Why?

16 Party Preparations

Mandy Sloane and Sandra Carter were making plans for having a party. They had finally recovered from the police most of the things that had been stolen from the flat, and the man who had burgled them was safely locked away in prison. It turned out that he was connected with over fifty burglaries that had taken place over the last six months! The two girls had been in their flat for long enough to feel that it was time they had a party, and the return of their radio, TV, and the rest of the things that had been stolen, gave them just the excuse they wanted.

'How much can we afford to spend on it then?' asked Sandra.

'Well,' replied Mandy, 'the rent's £16.50 a week between us, and my take-home wages are £33 per week. I'll need ten quid to see me through the week, and I can chip in what's left over.'

Sandra thought for a moment, then she said, 'I take home £31.00. After I've paid the rent, I'll need about eight pounds to last me till the next pay-day. How much does that give us altogether?'

Mandy grinned at her friend. 'I think we should have enough for a right old knees up,' she said.

The two of them worked out who they were going to invite, then they added up the numbers.

'We should end up with about twenty-four people, including ourselves,' said Mandy. 'What shall we do about drinks?'

'We could ask them to bring a bottle with them when they come,' Sandra suggested. 'What shall we buy to go with it?'

'You're the one what knows about booze,' replied Mandy. 'What do you think?'

'We'll stick to beer and cider, eh? Anyone who wants anything fancy can bring their own,' said Sandra.

'All right,' Mandy agreed. 'What about food?'

'We could do a big dish of rice and curry,' Sandra suggested. 'Most people like curry.'

'We'll do a big bowl of chopped salad and things too, eh?' said Mandy.

'That, with some cheese and biscuits should be enough.'

Sandra disagreed. 'I think we ought to do a bit more than that. I was thinking of some bits of cheese and pineapple on sticks, and some sausages on sticks, and some pickled onions.'

'You only want to get that lot so you can stuff it all yourself,' said Mandy, laughing.

They arranged their party for the following Saturday evening, and on the Saturday morning they went out shopping. First they went to the off-licence to buy the drinks.

'Look!' said Sandra. 'Cider is only 62 pence a flagon at this place. Let's get a dozen bottles.'

'O.K.' Mandy agreed. 'How about beer? Shall we get some of those big seven-pint cans? They're only £2.40 each.'

'How many shall we get then?' asked Sandra. 'Shall we get about ten?'

Mandy laughed. 'How do we get ten?' she asked. 'That would take more money than we got. We get five, O.K.?'

'Oh yeah,' said Sandra, feeling foolish. 'I wasn't thinking.'

The shopkeeper packed the drinks into a couple of cardboard boxes.

'That will be nineteen pounds and eighty-four pence, please,' said the shopkeeper.

Sandra was just about to pay him when Mandy stopped her.

'I think you've overcharged us, Mister,' she said.

The shopkeeper went red. 'No I 'aven't,' he said.

'Well just check it again would you?' asked Mandy.

The shopkeeper wrote down all the things that they had bought, then he added up the prices to find the total.

'Sorry, love,' he said. 'My mistake.'

The two girls paid him the correct price, then they left the shop together.

'Do you think he overcharged us on purpose?' Sandra asked Mandy.

'You got to watch that man,' Mandy told her. 'Last time I was in there, he tried to give me change of a pound for a fiver.'

They took the drinks home, then they went back to the shops. They stopped outside the butcher's and after inspecting the meat in his display, they went in.

'How much is that chuck steak?' Sandra asked the butcher.

'Eighty-five pence a pound, my lovely,' said the butcher.

'Give us two lovely pounds then,' said Sandra.

'All my meat's lovely here,' replied the butcher, grinning at them as he weighed it out.

'How much are your chipolata sausages?' asked Sandra, as he handed her the steak.

'Sixty pence a pound to you,' he replied.

They bought two and a half pounds of sausages, then they moved on to the grocer's.

At the grocer's, they bought two pounds of Cheddar cheese at 68 pence a pound; three packets of cheese biscuits that cost 36 pence each; two pounds of rice at 38 pence a pound; a large jar of pickled onions that were on offer at 43 pence; a big tin of pineapple pieces which cost 50 pence; and a pound of dried fruit for the curry and salad which cost them 64 pence.

'We haven't got much left,' said Sandra after they had paid the grocer.

'Ah, that's no problem,' Mandy told her. 'We've only got to get the salad things now and we're through.'

In the greengrocer's, they bought two big lettuces at 18 pence each; two pounds of apples at 28 pence a pound; two pounds of tomatoes at 27 pence a pound; a stick of celery which cost them 20 pence; and three bananas which came to 18 pence.

When they had finished paying the greengrocer, Sandra looked sadly into the purse which had held all their money for the party. 'Well, what's left in there isn't going to get us very far,' she said.

Mandy looked inside the purse. 'That's just about enough to buy a packet of those sticks for the cheese and pineapple and things you want to do,' she said. 'Come on. Let's get going. We've got a lot to do if we're going to have all that stuff ready for tonight.'

As they headed for home, laden down with their bags full of shopping, Sandra suddenly stopped. 'Oh naffing rotten hell!' she exclaimed. 'You know what we forgot don't you? We didn't get no salad cream.'

Mandy looked at her and smiled. 'That's not a problem,' she said. 'We got oil and vinegar and eggs at home. My mum showed me how to make salad dressing mixing egg yolk and olive oil with vinegar and mustard powder. It's just as good as anything you buy.'

Sandra looked at her and pulled a funny face. 'Right little Fanny Craddock aren't you?' she said.

The two girls laughed and continued on up the High Road towards their home.

Questions

1 How much rent does Sandra pay per week?
2 Including her rent money, how much does Sandra need to deduct from her wages before she can begin spending on the party?
3 Including her rent money, how much does Mandy need to

deduct from her wages before she can begin spending on the party?

4 How much will they have altogether that they can spend on the party?
5 How much does the cider that they buy come to?
6 How much would ten seven-pint cans of beer and twelve bottles of cider come to?
7 How much does the beer that they buy come to?
8 What should their bill in the off-licence come to?
9 By how much does the shopkeeper try to overcharge them?
10 What does Sandra buy in the butcher's?
11 How much should her bill come to in the butcher's?
12 How much should they have left after they've paid the butcher?
13 What is their bill in the grocer's shop?
14 What is their bill in the greengrocer's shop?
15 How much do they have left after they've paid the greengrocer?
16 What are the ingredients for Mandy's home-made salad dressing?

*   *   *

A If you had thirty pounds to spend on a party, what would you buy? Make out a list of what you would spend on what.
B How would you organise your party? Who would you invite? Would you make special arrangements to keep out gate-crashers? Describe how you would set about making the arrangements for your ideal party.
C What do you think of shop assistants who overcharge customers? Do you think they do it on purpose? What would you say if you found that you had been overcharged?
D If you were working in a shop, and someone accused you of overcharging them, what would you do? What would you say if you found that you had overcharged them?

17 The Party

It was eight o'clock on Saturday evening by the time that Sandra Carter and Mandy Sloane had finished all the preparations for their party. A big dish of golden curry and saffron rice was simmering in the oven, sending out lovely spicy smells that filled the flat. The table and sideboard in their sitting-room were covered with things to eat and drink. Plates of cold sausages and cheese and biscuits lay side by side with bowls of cheese and pineapple, jars of pickled onions, and a huge dish of mixed salad. A pile of cardboard plates and cups were stacked at the back of the sideboard, and gleaming bottles of cider and some big, seven-pint cans of beer were neatly arranged at the side of the food.

'Right. That's that,' said Mandy in satisfaction as she looked round their brightly-lit sitting-room. 'Everything looks fine now,' she said, 'but God knows what it will look like at the end of the evening.'

'I hope everyone comes,' said Sandra. 'It would be horrible if no one came.'

'Oh! Stop worrying,' Mandy replied impatiently. 'Everything'll be OK. You wait and see.'

'Shall we go out for a drink?' said Sandra. 'No one will be here for about an hour.'

'Could do,' Mandy answered.

'Come on,' Sandra grinned at her friend. 'I've worked up a real thirst, what with all this cooking and cleaning and getting dressed up, I could just do with a pint of lager.'

'You guts,' said Mandy as she put her coat on, 'you'll get as fat as a pig if you drink that much.'

'You worry about your own figure, and leave me to worry about mine mate,' Sandra answered, and the two of them went out.

The pub on the corner was fairly crowded as they walked in. Mandy was about to go up to the bar and order the drinks when she felt Sandra pull her arm.

'There's some of our lot over there,' said Sandra, indicating a group of their friends over in a corner of the room. 'Come on. Let's go over and join them. They'll buy us the drinks.'

'Good thinking, girl,' replied Mandy, and they moved over to greet their friends.

''Ere, look what the cat's brought in!' said Russell Bannerman as he saw them.

'Yeah, and look what the cat wouldn't touch,' Sandra replied mockingly.

''Ello girls,' said Winston Brown. 'What you 'aving to drink?'

Sandra looked at Mandy and winked. 'Thanks, Winston,' she said, 'I'll have a pint of lager.'

Mandy winked back at her. 'I'll have a Babycham please, Winston,' she said.

It was ten o'clock by the time that they returned to their flat, accompanied by their friends. By eleven, the party was in full swing. All the people who had been invited had arrived, and most of them had brought something along to drink. People were dancing and enjoying themselves in both of the rooms in the flat, and the record-player was turned up full volume. The flat was filled with noise and cigarette smoke, and the smells of perfume and hair laquer combined with sweat.

Sandra was dancing with her boyfriend Tommy when one of her friends came up and pulled at her sleeve.

'The bloke from the flat down below is at the door,' she said. 'He's complaining that the noise is too loud.'

'Oh blimey!' said Sandra. 'Hang on a minute. I'll go and talk to him.' The man from downstairs was standing at the door looking angry and red-faced. 'Would you mind turning down the noise?' he asked angrily. 'My wife is not well, and we're trying to sleep downstairs.'

'I'm ever so sorry,' Sandra replied. 'I'll turn it down right away. I'm terribly sorry.'

The man's grim expression softened for a moment, then returned as a voice from behind Sandra spoke out. It was Russell Bannerman.

'Ah push off, you silly old fool,' he said in a drunken, slurred voice. 'If you can't sleep, go and put your head in a gas oven, you raas clot!'

'Shut up, Russell!' snapped Sandra. She turned back to the man. 'I'm really sorry,' she said.

The man glared at Russell, then turned away and walked back down the stairs as the door of the flat closed behind him.

Sandra went over to the record-player and turned it down, then she went round all the people in the two rooms and asked them to keep the noise down because of the neighbours. When she went back into the other room she saw Russell Bannerman holding the door open to a group of teenagers who had just walked in. Two were black and two white. None of them were known to her. She moved across the room to face them.

'What do you want?' she said.

'We've come to the big party,' said one of them. He was the biggest of the group of four, with swept-back greasy hair and piggy eyes. He was wearing a yellow jacket with a big 'G' on it.

'Who invited you?' asked Sandra.

'We invited ourselves,' another of the boys replied. He took a big bottle of vodka from his pocket and drank from it.

Sandra moved back to Russell Bannerman. 'What did you let them in for?' she asked him angrily. 'They're just gatecrashers. Can you keep them here while I go and fetch Tommy?'

Russell looked at the four youths, then looked at the floor. 'I'm not feeling too good,' he mumbled.

'You're useless!' said Sandra. She went into the other room to look for Tommy. When she told him about the

gatecrashers, he went around the room and gathered together some of his friends. Six of them went into the next room and approached the group of gatecrashers who were now standing by the record-player.

'This is a private party,' said Tommy, facing up to them. 'I think you'd better go.'

'Oh yeah? Who's going to make us then?' asked the one with the vodka bottle. His mates moved up to stand on each side of him.

Just as it looked as if a fight was about to erupt and spoil the party altogether, there was a loud banging on the door of the flat.

'Open up!' said a loud voice. 'This is the police. Open the door!'

When Sandra opened the door, two big policemen walked into the room, followed by the man from the downstairs flat.

'Who is the tenant of this flat?' asked one of the policemen. He had a beard and a deep voice.

'Me,' said Sandra.

'And me,' said Mandy, stepping forward.

'Don't you know that it's an offence to create excessive noise after eleven o'clock?' said the bearded policeman. Then he caught sight of the four gatecrashers, who were trying to skulk away into a dark corner of the room. He peered at them closely. 'Come here into the light, you four,' he said.

The youths shuffled forwards slowly.

'They shouldn't be here really,' said Mandy quickly. 'They've just gatecrashed in, and they were about to start a fight.'

'I do believe it's our little friend Gooch,' said the other policeman, 'and he's wearing a yellow jacket.'

'Just like the lad who led the gang that attacked the manager of an off-licence tonight, and robbed him,' continued the bearded policeman.

'Come on, you four. Downstairs.' He turned back to face the girls and the other people in the room. 'You lot just keep the noise down,' he said, 'or we'll send the lot of you home and charge the tenants of the flat with causing a disturbance. Which is the one who insulted you?' he asked the man from the downstairs flat.

'That one,' replied the man, pointing at where Russell stood leaning against the wall.

'What me?' said Russell. 'I didn't do nothing.'

The policeman looked at Russell. 'Don't you think you'd better apologise?' he said. There was a pause.

'I didn't do nothing,' Russell whined.

'Get on home then, sunshine,' said the policeman after another pause. 'If you haven't got the guts to say sorry, you'd better get out, before we charge you with behaviour likely to cause a breach of the peace. Go on. Clear off.'

Looking down at the floor, Russell left the room. No one spoke.

'Come on then, let's go,' said the bearded policeman. The other one left the room first, followed by the four gatecrashers and the man from the downstairs flat. The bearded policeman left last.

After they had gone, the party picked up again, but this time there was less noise. Despite this, everyone still seemed to enjoy themselves, and the curry which the girls had prepared disappeared quickly down hungry throats. By the time that the party came to an end, when most people had gone home, it was half-past three in the morning!

Sandra looked around the room at the empty plates and the squashed paper cups; at the cigarette ash on the carpets and the bits of food dropped here and there and trodden into the floor; and at the litter of empty bottles that were scattered all over the place.

'Ugh!' she said. 'What a mess!'

Tommy yawned. 'Don't bother about that now,' he said. 'Leave it until the morning.'

'It's a good job the police arrived when they did,' Sandra remarked. 'If Russell hadn't been so rude to that man downstairs, maybe they wouldn't have come at all.'

'Russell,' said Tommy slowly, 'is a total waste of time. Still,' he continued, 'sometimes a waste of time can be useful.'

Questions

1 What is Sandra worrying about at the start of the evening?
2 What does Mandy say will happen to Sandra if she drinks a lot?
3 Why does Sandra stop Mandy from going up to the bar?
4 What time is it by the time the party gets into full swing?
5 Who complains about the noise?
6 Why does he want them to keep the noise down?
7 What does the man do after Russell speaks to him?
8 What does Mandy do after the man leaves?
9 Describe what you know of the appearance of the gatecrashers.
10 What does Sandra ask Russell to do about the gatecrashers?
11 What does Tommy do when he is told about the gatecrashers?
12 What do the gatecrashers do when Tommy asks them to leave?
13 Who do you think called the police, and why?
14 What kind of offence does the policeman tell Mandy and Sandra that they are committing?
15 What is the offence that the police suspect the gatecrashers have committed?
16 Why do the police connect the gatecrashers with this crime?
17 With what does the policeman threaten to charge the tenants of the flat?
18 With what does the policeman threaten to charge Russell?
19 Why does the policeman throw Russell out of the party?
20 Describe the state of the flat after the party is over.

*   *   *

What preparations would you make if you wanted to have a good party in a flat like Sandra's, without having any trouble?

18 Two Old Men

Tommy Brown jumped off the 'bus in Battersea and walked through the evening sunshine along Lavender Hill. The rush hour had just finished, but there were still quite a few people around. Tommy walked along the pavement whistling to himself and thinking about what he was going to do that evening. After he'd had tea, he thought that he might go over to Clapham Common and have a game of football. It was either that, or go round to see his cousin Jimmy and maybe go to a film. His thoughts were disturbed by a familiar voice at the side of him.

'Wotcher, Tom,' said the voice.

Tommy turned to face the speaker in surprise. It was Anthony Roach.

'Hullo, Tony,' he said, grinning with pleasure at seeing his friend.

'Where did you spring from?'

'I thought it was you from behind, so I ran to catch up with you,' said Anthony, falling into step beside him. 'How's it going?'

'Oh, same as usual,' Tommy replied. 'How about you?'

'Yeah. All right,' said Anthony. 'How's the new job then?'

'It's fair enough,' Tommy answered, 'better than the queer place anyway.'

'Do you fancy a quick drink?' asked Anthony. 'I'm dying of thirst. I've been plastering all afternoon.'

'Yeah, now you come to mention it, so am I,' said Tommy.

The two friends dived into the first pub that they came to, and walked up to the bar.

'What are you having then?' Tommy asked his friend.

'I'll have a pint of shandy,' Anthony replied, 'seeing as you're in the money.'

'You must be joking,' Tommy answered.

The barman served their drinks. A pint of shandy cost 38 pence, and a pint of bitter was 36p. Tommy gave the barman a pound note and checked his change, then they moved across the bar and sat down at a table near the window.

'What's happening at Community Industry then?' asked Tommy, after taking a swig at his beer.

'Nothing much,' Anthony replied. 'Except Russell Bannerman's brother has started. Errol Bannerman. He's just as stupid as Russell. He threw a mallet at Winston Lewis yesterday.'

'Typical,' said Tommy in disgust.

Their attention was distracted by a deep voice at the table next to them saying, 'I'm sure it's him.' The speaker was a big, barrel-chested man who was sitting with three old ladies, and staring hard across the room. From the wrinkles on the man's face, it was obvious that he was an old man, but with his fine build and his black, wavy hair, he looked like a man in his fifties. He was certainly a very striking old man.

'He's a tasty old geezer, isn't he?' said Tommy quietly to Anthony. The two youths watched the man as he carried his drink across the room to where an old man was sitting alone at a table.

In contrast to the big man, the other old man looked as if he was on his last legs. He was shrunken and bald, and two walking sticks were resting on the back of his chair. He was sitting hunched up and grey-faced, looking miserably at the half-pint of bitter on the table in front of him, as though he was just having a last drink before he died and didn't want to hurry it.

The big man stood for a moment looking carefully at the old man sitting before him, then he spoke. 'All right, old timer?' he said. The old man looked up. 'Yes, thank you.' He spoke in a thin, weedy voice.

'He could have fooled me,' Tommy whispered to Anthony.

He looks like he's dead and buried, but no one's had the heart to tell him yet,' Anthony replied laughing.

'Feeling your age, eh?' said the big man.

The old man looked up at him for a moment and took a drink from his beer before replying. 'You might say that,' he said.

'Comes to us all in the end,' said the big man. 'Not like the good old days, eh?'

'You can say that again,' replied the old man. A thin-lipped smile, like that of a lizard, creased his face for an instant, then vanished.

'Were you an army man?' the big man asked him.

'Yes,' replied the other, livening up a bit. 'How did you know?'

'I looked at you,' said the big man, 'and I says to meself, "There's an ex-army man." Those were the days! Young and strong and fit to fight a lion. I could eat a table in those days. Who were you with?'

'Eighth Army,' replied the old man, his eyes glittering at the memory. 'Who were you with?'

'Me? I was a Navy man meself. Merchant Navy. Did fifteen years,' the big fellow replied. He finished his drink, then said to the other, 'Let me buy you a drink.'

'Thanks very much,' he said, draining his half pint glass. 'I'll have a pint of the best.'

The big man smiled and moved up to the bar. He returned to the old man's table with two pints of bitter, then went back to the bar and carried a tray of drinks over to the table where the old ladies were sitting.

'What are you up to, Bill?' one of them asked him.

'Nothing much,' replied the big man with a wink at them. 'It's him all right, but he doesn't know who I am.' He walked back to the table where the old man sat sipping his beer, and he sat down at the table with him. He raised his glass. 'Cheers,' he said.

'Your good health,' replied the old man, raising his glass.

'How old are you then?' the big man asked him suddenly.

After a pause, the old man replied, 'Sixty-two. How old are you?'

'How old do you think I am?' he answered.

'Mmmm. I should say about sixty, sixty-five,' said the old man.

'Would you?' the big man retorted. He seemed very pleased. 'I'm eighty-four,' he announced proudly. 'Don't look it, do I?'

'No,' said the other glumly.

The big man seemed to enjoy the other's obvious jealousy of him. He smiled broadly for a moment, then he said sharply, 'You used to be a policeman, didn't you?'

The old man was obviously startled. 'How do you know?' he asked.

'I don't forget, mate,' said the big man in a rather threatening tone of voice. 'You thought I'd forgotten you years ago, I bet. Do you remember the Cup Final back in 1952? There you were, up there on your big white horse, shoving us about like cattle. You nicked me for calling you names, didn't you? Insulting behaviour you called it. Back at the Station, there you were, laughing away at me with all your horrible little mates. I told you I'd see you again, and now I have. Look where your nasty little ways have got you now.'

The old man looked at him, saying nothing.

'This is what living clean does for you, mate,' said the big man, thumping on his powerful chest with one hand. 'Look at you, you poor old bugger. That's what all your sneaking and creeping does for you.'

The old man looked at him piercingly for a moment longer, then he rose to his feet in silence. Picking up his walking sticks, he hobbled to the door, leaving his drink half-finished on the table behind him. He looked sad and lonely as he passed through the door: a broken old man on his way to the grave.

The big man watched him go with a smile of grim satisfaction, then he rejoined his party.

'You shouldn't have done that, Bill,' said one of the old ladies.

'No, you shouldn't have, Bill,' another agreed with her. 'That was mean that was. Pretending to be friendly like that, then upsetting him.'

'Ah, get away with you,' the big man replied. 'He was a right 'orrible sort of bloke when I knew him then, and I bet he still is now.'

'Come on,' said Tommy to his friend, 'let's get going.' They finished their drinks and left the pub.

'That was funny, wasn't it?' said Anthony as they went outside.

'I dunno,' said Tommy thoughtfully. 'I dunno if it was funny or not.'

Questions

1 What is the rush hour, and when does it usually occur?
2 What does Tommy think of doing that evening?
3 What has Anthony been doing to make him so thirsty?
4 How much change would Tommy get from a pound after paying for his and Anthony's drink?
5 Who has just started work at Community Industry, and why does Anthony call him stupid?
6 What does the big man look like?
7 Who is the big man with?
8 What does the old man look like?
9 What do people mean when they talk about 'the good old days?'
10 What part of the Armed Forces did the old man serve in?
11 In what ways does the big man exaggerate?

12 What did the big man serve in?
13 How much would two pints of bitter cost?
14 What are the ages of the two men?
15 Describe some of the other differences between the two men.
16 Why would the old man be jealous of the other one?
17 Why does the big man have a grudge against the other?
18 What does the big man blame the other's pitiful appearance on?
19 What does the old man leave behind him as he goes?
20 What do the man's friends say about what he does to the old man? Do you agree with them? Give your reasons.

   *   *   *   ,

A Many people hold grudges for a long time. Do they serve any useful purpose? Give examples of any useful purposes you think they might serve, and other examples of the harmful effects of holding a grudge.
B Do people become more sensible as they get older? Give reasons to support your opinions.
C Can you see any similarity between the actions of the big man towards the other, and the actions which he says the old man took against him when he was a policeman? Does this story make you think that one of the old men is preferable to the other? Why?
D Write a short story called 'The Grudge.'
E Write a follow-up story in which the two men meet again.

19 Getting into Trouble

'Come on. Get another pint down you,' Russell Bannerman urged his friend, Jimmy Brown.

'That's all right with me,' said Jimmy, slurring his speech a little.

'You're the one who's in for the next round.'

'Give us yer glass then,' Russell told him, then he shouted to the barman to bring another two pints of extra strong bitter.

The two of them were standing at the bar of a pub over in Putney. The place was crowded and noisy, full of tobacco smoke and conversation, and getting more and more noisy as it moved towards closing time. The two friends had gone over there to celebrate Russell's first pay-packet from his new job, working in a warehouse. Neither of them were new to drinking, but both of them had drunk far more than they were used to, and were each feeling quite drunk.

'Here's to it – whatever it is,' said Russell, raising his brimming glass at his friend.

'Cheers, Russ,' replied Jimmy, swaying slightly on his heels. He felt really fine, but a bit light-headed, and he was full of admiration for Russell's generosity. Russell seemed to be a really good bloke. He had bought Jimmy at least eight pints of beer that evening, although Jimmy was supposed to pay him back when he got paid on the following Friday. 'You're a really good bloke, you are, Russ,' he said, in a burst of drunken sincerity.

Russell grinned at him over his glass. 'You ain't so bad yerself,' he replied, 'even if you do blow your nose in the blankets.'

Jimmy sniggered into his beer. Everything seemed to be warm and friendly, and he felt confident and able to cope with anything. If anyone tried to pick a fight, he thought, he could handle them with no trouble. He looked around to see if anyone was looking at him. A man was staring vaguely in his direction. Jimmy stared the man full in the face, feeling his stomach tighten as he anticipated trouble. The man looked away in another direction, and Jimmy relaxed. He took a long pull at his glass of beer, and was surprised to find that it was almost empty once again.

'Goes down a treat, don't it?' said Russell, putting his own glass down empty. He reached into his pocket for his wallet. 'One more pint, and that makes it ten you owe me.'

'Yeah. Great. That's really good of you, mate,' said Jimmy. He drained his glass and handed it to Russell. Someone nudged him from behind. Jimmy turned around, ready for a fight. 'Who do you think you're pushing into mate,' he said, as he tried to focus his eyes onto the man facing him.

'Sorry about that, pal,' said a lazy, unconcerned voice. It was the man whom Jimmy had thought was staring at him.

'You will be in a minute,' said Jimmy, feeling confident that the man was afraid of him.

The man looked him steadily in the eyes. 'What do you mean by that then, sunshine?' he asked, his voice taking on a sharper edge.

Jimmy felt a bit less sure of himself. 'You just want to watch it. That's all,' he said.

'You better step outside then me old son,' replied the man. 'Someone ought to teach you to watch your manners.' He was standing facing Jimmy squarely, looking him straight in the eyes, his lips set in a thin line in his white face.

'All right, all right. There's no need to lose your rag,' said Jimmy. 'I was only asking you not to bump into me.'

'Oh yeah?' said the man, elbowing him aside as he moved up to the bar. Russell moved around to join him with the drinks. 'Let's get away from the bar,' he said. 'It's crowded up here.'

'That bloke was getting really moody,' complained

Jimmy, feeling annoyed with himself and the man who had nudged him.

'Aw, you don't want to worry about people like that,' said Russell. 'Just ignore him.'

Jimmy took a big swig at his glass of beer. 'I'm not having people going on at me like that,' he said.

'Just forget it man,' Russell told him. 'It's not worth it.'

'It's all right for you to say that,' said Jimmy. 'He wasn't talking to you.'

When they went outside into the fresh air, Jimmy suddenly made up his mind that he was going to have it out with the man. He waited outside the pub until he came out, with Russell waiting for him on the opposite side of the road. When the man appeared, Jimmy walked up to him. 'You want trouble then, mate?' he said.

The next thing he knew, he was sitting in a shop doorway, with Russell squatting at his side. His mouth felt swollen and painful, and as he ran his tongue along his top lip, he felt his front teeth were broken.

'I told you to forget it,' said Russell. 'That bloke was greased lightning.'

Jimmy spoke with difficulty through his broken teeth. 'Good laugh though, wannit?' he said. He felt curiously unconcerned about it all, and he was still warm and glowing inside. He got to his feet. 'Come on,' he said. 'Let's make tracks for home.'

The two of them made their way along Putney High Street, going up towards the station. Suddenly Russell darted down an alley at the side of a shop. 'Just going for a leak,' he called back.

Jimmy moved down the alley behind him. 'I think I'll join you,' he said, speaking thickly through his damaged mouth.

Standing facing a blank brick wall, Jimmy let his eyes wander upwards. He suddenly realised that he was looking at an open window just above him. He felt dazed and happy, and he wanted to impress Russell after his defeat by the unknown man earlier. 'Give us a leg up, Russ,' he said. 'This looks like a good laugh.'

The fresh air seemed to have hit Russell too, and he joined in the idea enthusiastically. 'No, I'll go up first,' he said. 'I'll pull you up from inside.' He clambered up the wall and vanished through the window.

Before he really knew what he was doing, Jimmy found himself standing beside Russell in a darkened store room at the back of what was obviously an electrical shop. The glow from the street lamps outside provided a faint light for them to see their surroundings. All around them were boxes and television sets; radios and stereo equipment. Jimmy started to giggle, and Russell joined in. It all seemed so hilariously funny. Their laughter grew louder and louder, and when Russell said, 'Ssh!' it only made them laugh even louder still.

When their laughter had subsided a bit, they moved into the main showroom at the front of the shop, and started looking around among the goods on display.

'We could make a fortune if we could get some of this stuff out of here,' said Jimmy. 'This colour TV costs three 'undred and fifty notes!'

'There's a stereo here for six 'undred,' replied Russell. 'What a laugh if we could get a load of this away.'

Jimmy picked up a calculator and put it in his pocket. 'I've always fancied one of them little pocket computer jobs,' he told Russell.

'I fancy a little radio meself,' replied Russell, picking up a small transistor radio from its stand in the window. 'I reckon we best get out of it now,' he said. 'The old Bill might be doing his rounds soon.' Jimmy felt like the room was beginning to spin a little. 'Yeah, let's get out then, eh?'

Russell dropped from the window out into the alley first, and Jimmy was just climbing out into the fresh air when he was caught in the beam of a torch. Russell moved back and tried to hide in the shadows, while Jimmy froze, half of him

hanging from outside the window, and the other half still inside the shop. He wriggled free after a moment, and dropped to the ground to join Russell in the alley as a voice rang out from behind the torch beam.

'You're nicked,' said the voice, holding the torch-beam on them squarely.

'Don't try to make a run for it, there's good lads. We got a couple of dogs here.'

Jimmy and Russell stood still in the bright ring of the torch-beam. It all seemed quite unreal to Jimmy, like it was some kind of strange dream. He suddenly had a funny idea. He grabbed hold of Russell's arm, and began to dance in the ring of light, saying, 'Hey Russell, we're on the stage! The spotlight is on us!' He began to sing as he danced, singing, 'Please release me, let me go . . .' The two of them started laughing again.

Two shadows moved up on them through the alley, and Jimmy felt himself suddenly being held in a strong grip as he was propelled towards the street light. He started to struggle, and felt a stab of pain as his arm was twisted up behind his back. 'Come along quietly, sonny,' said the voice holding him. 'Any trouble, and you'll be done for resisting arrest and assaulting a police officer.'

Everything stopped being funny to Jimmy from that point onwards. It wasn't funny when he was sick all over his clothes on the way to the police station, and it wasn't funny when he had his fingerprints taken and had to sit in a bare room for what seemed like ages making a statement. What especially wasn't funny was spending three weeks in a remand centre, while he waited for his case to come up before a Crown court. That wasn't funny, and neither was the six months suspended sentence that he received when he finally did appear in Court. Having six months in nick hanging over his head for the next two years didn't strike him as being any kind of a laugh at all.

Questions

1 What are Jimmy and Russell celebrating?
2 When does Jimmy have to pay Russell back?
3 Why does Jimmy look around the pub?
4 How many pints does Russell buy Jimmy altogether?
5 Why does Jimmy try to pick a fight in the pub?
6 Do you think that Jimmy or the other man is in the wrong? Why?
7 What is Russell's advice to Jimmy about the man, and others like him?
8 Do you think Russell's advice is good or bad? Why?
9 What does Jimmy do as soon as he leaves the pub'?
10 How is Jimmy injured as a result of his behaviour towards the man?
11 Why do Jimmy and Russell go into the shop?
12 What kind of a shop is it?
13 How do the two of them see their way around the shop?
14 What is the combined value of the colour TV and the stereo set?
15 What does Jimmy steal from the shop?
16 What does Russell steal from the shop?
17 What does the policeman say will happen to Jimmy if he makes any trouble?
18 Why does Jimmy spend three weeks in a Remand Centre?
19 What is Jimmy's sentence?
20 Do you think that Jimmy got off lightly for his evening's activities? What else might have happened to him as a result of his behaviour?

* * *

A Do you think that people who break the law in this country are treated lightly or severely? Give reasons for your opinion.
B Would you like to see any other forms of punishment for crime being introduced in this country, other than those which exist at present? If so, what kinds of punishment?
C What kind of crimes do you associate with drunkenness? Should there be a limit on the amount that people are allowed to drink?
D Write an essay called 'Crime and Punishment.'

20 On Holiday in Spain

Sandra Carter yawned as she and Mandy Sloane went down the stairs of their Spanish hotel on the first day of their holiday. The excitement leading up to their departure, followed by the rush to catch their 'plane, the flight to Malaga, and the long drive by coach to their hotel from the airport, had left them completely exhausted. All of them had gone straight to bed as soon as they had arrived at their hotel. Now, with the morning sun shining down outside, Sandra felt happy and excited, thinking about what her first day in a foreign country was going to be like.

'*Buenos dias Señoritas*,' said a white-jacketed waiter, smiling at them as he passed them on their way to the dining room.

The two girls giggled.

''Ere, what's he on about?' said Sandra.

'Don't ask me,' laughed Mandy in reply.

They found a vacant table in the dining room, where they were soon joined by their boyfriends, Winston Lewis and Tommy Brown.

'This is the life,' said Winston, as they ate a breakfast of juicy, ripe melon and crusty bread and jam, washed down with hot coffee. 'I ain't never had melon for breakfast before.'

'Me neither,' said Tommy. 'It's good innit?'

By the time that they had finished breakfast, had a shower, and got ready to go to the beach, it was way past ten o'clock. Stepping out of their shady, air-conditioned hotel into the bright Spanish sunlight, the heat hit them like a blast from an oven.

'Blimey! It's boiling!' exclaimed Mandy.

'It's not exactly cold, is it,' said Winston. 'I feel like lying down in the sun already.'

Mandy sniffed. 'You wanting to lie down is nothing new,' she said.

Winston looked at her and rolled his eyes. 'Raasclaat,' he muttered.

'We'll have to watch that sun, Sandra,' said Tommy. 'You'd better have something with you to cover your shoulders, or you'll burn summat wicked.'

'I got me cotton jacket in me bag,' Sandra replied. 'It's all right for you two,' she said to Winston and Mandy, 'you don't have to worry about being burned.'

'You must be joking!' replied Mandy. 'We burn as easy as you do. It's the same business of getting your skin used to sunlight, don't matter if you're black or white.'

They made their way through narrow, cobbled streets, lined with white-painted houses with wooden shutters on the windows, and cool and shady cafés, from which came delicious smells of savoury food. When they arrived at the beach, they found themselves an empty place up on some rocks, away from the bulk of the people. Tommy was the first to dive into the water.

'Blimey!' he shouted up at them. 'It's as warm as a bath at home! It's great!'

Soon all four of them were splashing around in the clear, blue Mediterranean sea. A lot of other people were out, swimming and diving in the water, and the four friends watched with interest as a youth with a face-mask and a snorkel tube walked from the water holding a spear gun, on the end of which wriggled a small octopus.

'I'm going to get some of that underwater swimming gear,' panted Winston to Tommy, as they came out of the water and flopped down onto the hot rocks to dry off.

'Same here,' replied Tommy. 'It's as clear as tap-water isn't it? I could see loads of fish swimming about beneath us by the rocks. It's great isn't it?'

'I never thought it'd be this warm,' said Mandy as she flopped down beside them. 'That breeze is like a flippin' hair dryer.'

They all lay basking in the sun for half an hour, then Winston nudged Tommy. 'I reckon that's about it for our dose of sun for today, isn't it? Any more on the first day out, and we're bound to burn.'

'Right,' said Tommy, stretching as he rose to his feet. 'That's your lot for today girls. You can do double time tomorrow.'

'What are we going to do now then?' asked Sandra as they all got dressed.

'Let's go and have a drink and something to eat,' said Winston. 'All that swimming has given me an appetite.'

'Good thinking, Batman,' Tommy said by way of a reply.

The four of them made their way up from the beach, sweating slightly in the hot sunlight. They went up a shaded side street away from the main road, and dived into the first café they found that looked reasonably cheap. Inside it was cool and almost empty, except for a couple of local workmen who were playing some kind of board game over in one corner.

'*Buenos dias,*' said a smiling man from behind the bar, then he said something else that they didn't understand.

'No understando,' said Tommy, feeling stupid. He thought that if he added an 'o' onto the end of what he said, it would somehow be more understandable. 'We Englisho,' he said.

'Ah! Good morning. How are you? What you like to drink?' said the man, smiling even more broadly. 'You like some sangria?'

'What's that?' asked Winston.

'A little brandy, plenty wine, tonic water, fruit, and plenty, plenty ice,' said the man. 'Iss very good. You like it.'

'That sounds great,' said Mandy. 'Let's try some of that.'

'Yeah. We'll have some of that, please,' said Tommy.

'What've you got to eat?' asked Winston. 'Have you got any pies or anything?'

'Food?' asked the man. 'You want food?'

'Yeah, food,' replied Winston. 'What do you have?'

'We got fried squid, octopus, paella . . .'

'What's that pyeller?' asked Sandra. 'I've heard of that.'

'Iss very good Spanish food. Pieces of fish, shrimps, mussels, squid, cooked in wine with rice and peppers. Iss very good. Very cheap,' said the man. He smiled at them broadly as he waited for their reply, showing his gold-capped front teeth.

'Is that all right with you then girls?' asked Tommy. 'It sounds like a good laugh to me.'

'You can only die once,' said Mandy.

'Yeah, stick your neck out,' said Winston. 'It might stop your head from falling off.'

'You want paella for four and sangria?' asked the man.

'Yes, please,' Tommy replied.

'I'm looking forward to this,' said Sandra as they waited. 'I wonder what it'll be like, that squid and that.'

'It sounded great didn't it?' Mandy answered. 'All that stuff cooked in wine should be terrific.'

The man with gold teeth brought them a huge clay jug that seemed to be stuffed with fruit and ice-cubes. Tilting the jug, he filled up four tall glasses which misted with cold as the deep red liquid gurgled out, along with chunks of ice and slices of apple and orange.

'Mmm,' said Sandra as she tasted it. 'This is really nice isn't it?'

'It's fantastic,' said Tommy. 'I hope it's not too expensive.'

Their meal, when it arrived, was as good, if not better than the drink. It looked like a multi-coloured curry, with yellow rice, green and red peppers, tomatoes, onions, and all kinds of different sea-food.

'This is one of the nicest things I've ever eaten,' said Tommy as he took a break from eating to drink some sangria.

'Yeah. Right,' said Winston, through a mouthful of food.

'Don't be a pig Winston,' said Mandy. 'We know what we're eating. You don't have to show us what it looks like all chewed up.'

'I'm going to make a right pig of myself,' Sandra announced, 'if all the food is as good as this.'

'That shouldn't be too hard,' said Tommy. 'You're fat enough as it is.'

At the end of the meal, they sat back feeling too full to move.

'How much does that lot come to then?' asked Tommy.

'About ten quid I expect,' grumbled Winston.

'Iss six hundred pesetas,' said the man with gold teeth.

'How much?' asked Winston. 'That sounds like a fortune!'

'Relax,' said Tommy after a moment. 'It's only just over four quid.'

'Is it?' exclaimed Winston, his face lighting up. 'Let's have some more of that sangreller or whatever it's called then.'

When they finally left the café, they decided to return to their hotel in order to drop off their wet swimming things, before going out to have a good look round the town. By the time that they got back to their hotel, however, they found that the combination of food and wine and hot sunshine had left them all feeling rather sleepy.

'I reckon I fancy a kip,' said Tommy, smothering a yawn.

'Me too,' said Winston. 'That sangreller makes you sleepy, don't it?'

'Well let's go to bed for an hour or two,' said Sandra, 'and we can meet up at, say, three o'clock.'

'Fair enough,' agreed Mandy.

Winston caught hold of her hand and pulled her away from the others.

'See you later then,' he said, grinning.

'Stop pulling at me, Winston,' Mandy told him as he led her away. She turned to smile back at Tommy and Sandra. 'See you in a bit then.'

Sandra and Tommy smiled back, and moved off towards the room shared by the two girls.

They met up again at three o'clock as they had agreed, and went out to have a look over the town. There were lots of souvenir shops and shops selling leather goods, as well as familiar-looking supermarkets and bakeries. When they tried to buy some underwater swimming equipment, they found that the shop-assistant didn't speak a word of English, but she wrote down the price of the face-masks and snorkel tubes that they wanted, so they knew how much to pay her. They found a huge, barn-like place, lined with rows of barrels, which sold all kinds of wine and spirits on draught, and they learned that this was called a bodega, although they didn't actually go into it. At the far end of the beach, they found a group of fishermen mending nets and passing a bottle of wine around among themselves, talking and joking as they worked.

As the four friends moved back down along the main beach, Winston suddenly pointed to a neon sign.

'Look at that!' he said. 'Fish and chips.'

They looked in at the window of the restaurant as they came level with it, and Tommy snorted in disgust.

'Have you seen how much they want for fish and chips?' he said. 'It's a hundred and fifty pesetas a portion! I think we'd better stick to local food.'

And so they did.

Questions

1 What had caused them to be so exhausted on their arrival at the hotel?
2 What do you imagine *Buenos dias* means?
3 Do you think that if you go to visit a foreign country, you should take the trouble to learn a little of the language? Give your reasons.
4 What do they have for breakfast?
5 What does Tommy tell Sandra that she will need in the sun?
6 What special equipment does the youth with the octopus have?
7 How long do they sunbathe for on the first day?
8 How long can they sunbathe for on the following day?
9 What do you think would happen to them if they lay in the sun for a few hours on this first day?
10 What does Winston want to do after they have finished sunbathing?
11 What kind of café do they go to?
12 Who is in the café?
13 Why does Tommy add an 'o' onto the end of what he says to the Spaniard?
14 What are the ingredients of sangria?
15 What are the ingredients of paella?
16 If you were abroad, would you like to try local food and drink that you had never had before, or would you try to stick to the things you know already? Give your reasons.
17 If six hundred pesetas is just over four pounds, approximately how many pesetas are there to the pound at the time of their visit to Spain?
18 What is it that makes them feel so sleepy?
19 What do they buy, and how do they find out how much they have to pay?
20 What is the price of Spanish fish and chips in English money?

✻   ✻   ✻

A If you could go on holiday anywhere in the world, where would you choose to go, and why would you go to that place in particular?
B Write a story in which you describe your ideal day on holiday in your ideal place.
C Write a story in which you get into some kind of trouble through not being able to speak the local language.